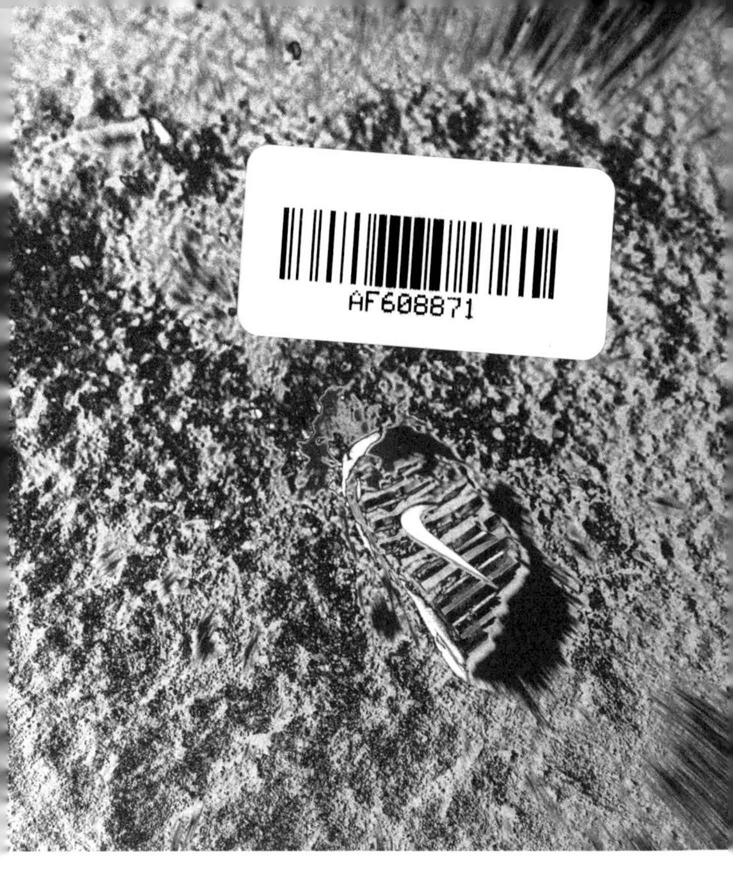

**If there are limits to
what we can do,
I don’t know what they are.**

No Finish Line

This book was first published in Nike's 50th year.

Design: Zak Group
Executive Editor: Sara Jhanjee
Editors: Sam Grawe, Jay Paavonpera, and Nick Schonberger
Essays: Sam Grawe
Fiction: Geoff Manaugh

Image Treatment: PWR
Image Research: Federico Sargentone
Illustration: Bráulio Amado

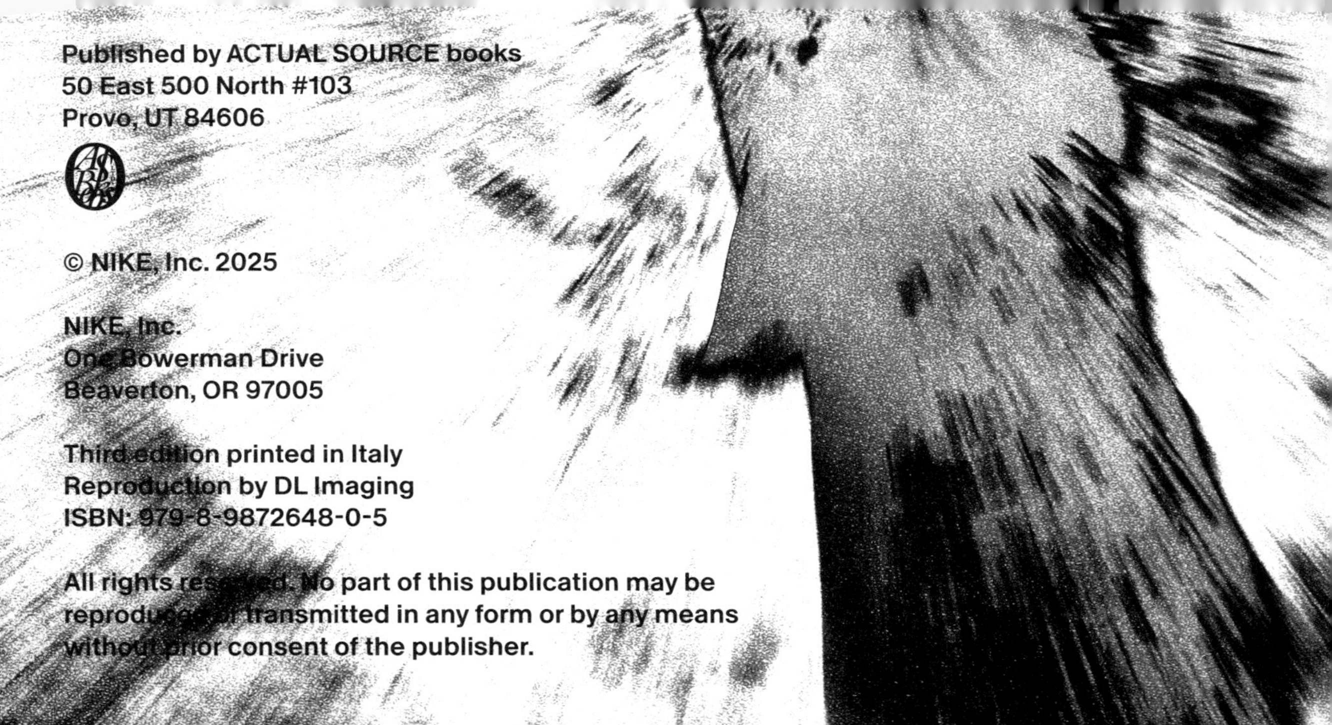

Published by ACTUAL SOURCE books
50 East 500 North #103
Provo, UT 84606

NIKE, Inc.
One Bowerman Drive
Beaverton, OR 97005

Third edition printed in Italy
Reproduction by DL Imaging
ISBN: 979-8-9872648-0-5

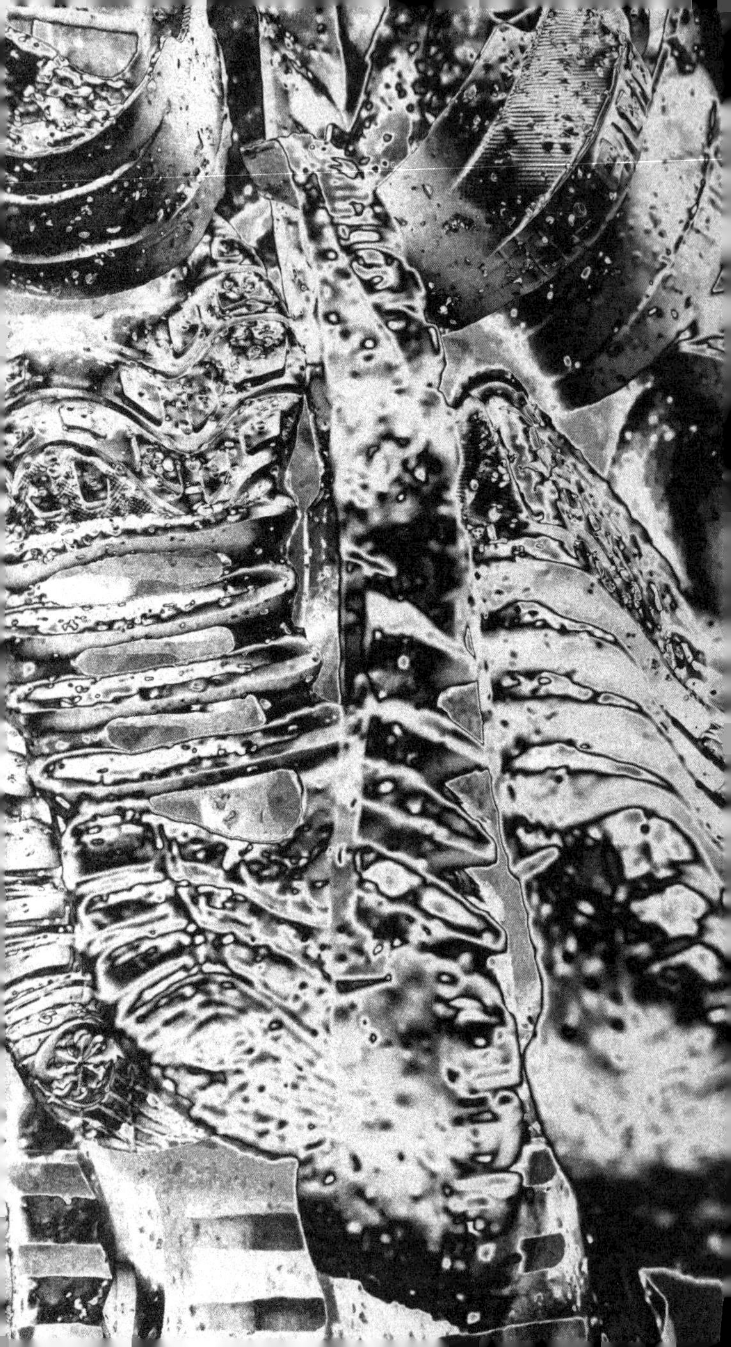

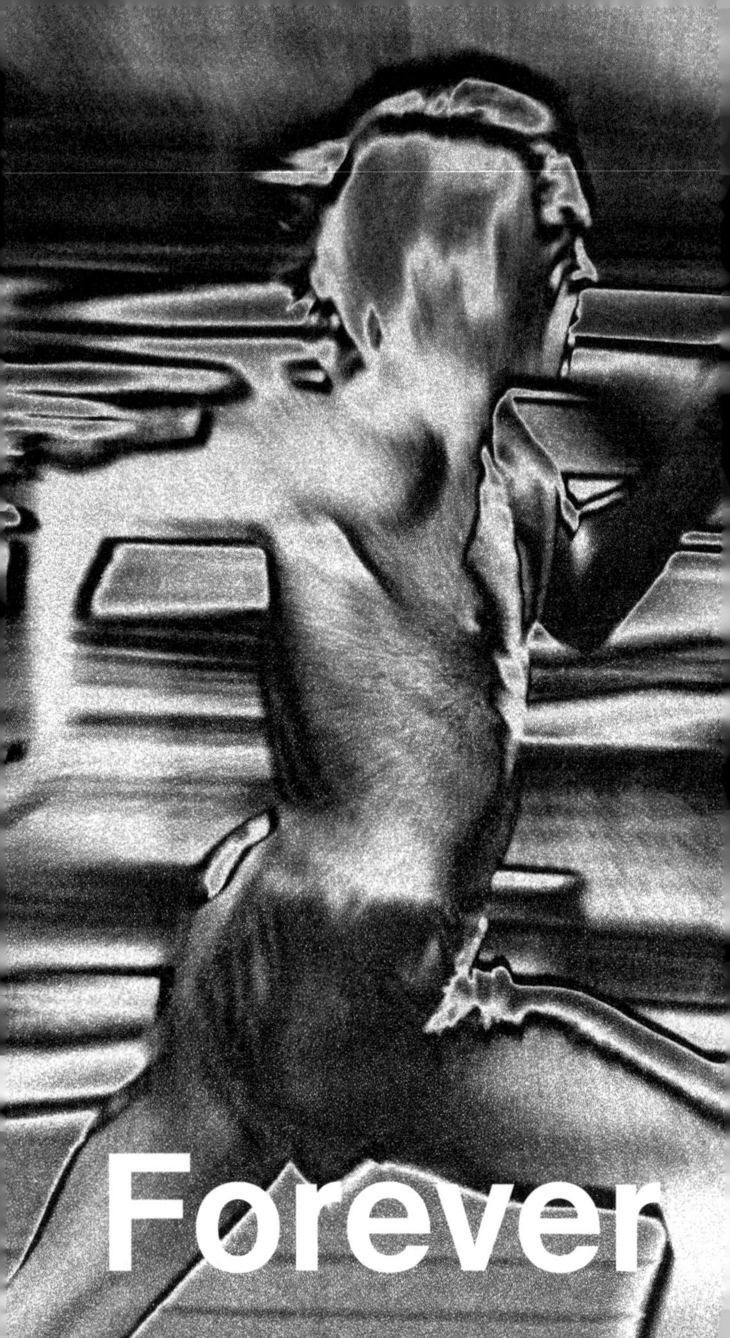
Forever

It's been said that the best way to predict the future is to create it. At Nike, we wholeheartedly agree. For over 50 years, we've endeavored to create a better future for athletes. This compels us forward, always. When we say, "There is no finish line," it's not a lazy reference to an unending grind or destination-less journey, but rather an expression of our belief in the limitless potential of sport — and design.

Nike's creative telescope to the future rests on three steadfast and guiding truths: we exist to match our athletes' dreams and ambitions; the progression of sport requires audacious imagination; and one innovation can ultimately benefit millions. In other words, when it comes to serving athletes, there's no problem too large or too small. With these truths in sight, we remain fixed on amplifying athletic ability, advancing human potential, and inviting everyone — and, importantly, every *body* — to experience sport for themself.

Creative progress at Nike is both evolutionary and revolutionary. As such, we are dedicated to continually iterating and improving demonstrated solutions as well as imagining and manifesting completely original ideas that force a reappraisal of what's possible. Every exploration is conceived in an unrelenting pursuit of better by design.

forward.

Nothing symbolizes the enduring ethos of endless progression and limitless potential more clearly than our iconic orange shoebox. More than simply a container, our humble shoebox is an invitation and also something more transcendent. It is a portal: a portal to generations of Nike know-how gained by listening, observing, hypothesizing, hustling, trialing, failing, succeeding, scaling, only to start all over again. The simple shoebox tethers us to where we started and suggests infinite unexamined possibilities.

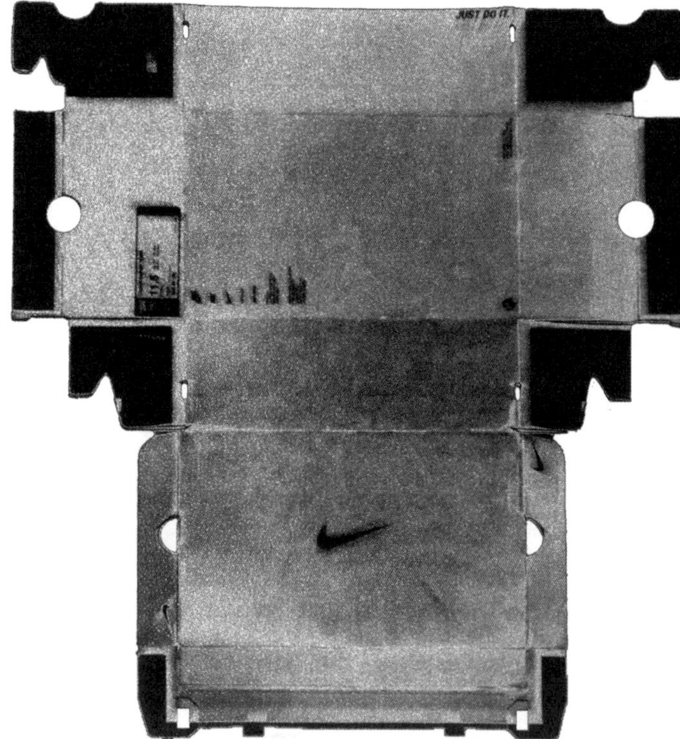

When our athletes unbox a new pair of shoes, they unbox much more than a final product.

They unbox a legacy.
An advantage.
Their potential.
The future of sport.

As we look to the next 50 years of Nike, the aperture, reach, and impact of that portal only expands. Together, we will build upon our shared legacy. We'll inspire and instigate progressive change on and off the playing field. We'll maintain a healthy disregard for the status quo and the barriers that enforce it. And, as always, we will dream big — as athletes and designers. In essence, we will shape a better world through sport by simply daring to create it.

I write this as Nike's Chief Design Officer, but I was once a kid daydreaming in a public pool who came up with an idea for a footwear-cushioning innovation inspired by the raft I was floating on. The idea felt promising enough that I drew it up and mailed it to someone named Phil Knight in Oregon. Design will change, but the need for human creativity and connection will not. Athletes and sport will continue to progress our understanding of each other and ourselves. And Nike will be there, designing every step of the way.

John Hoke III
Chief Design Officer, NIKE, Inc.

Design is inherently directed toward the future.

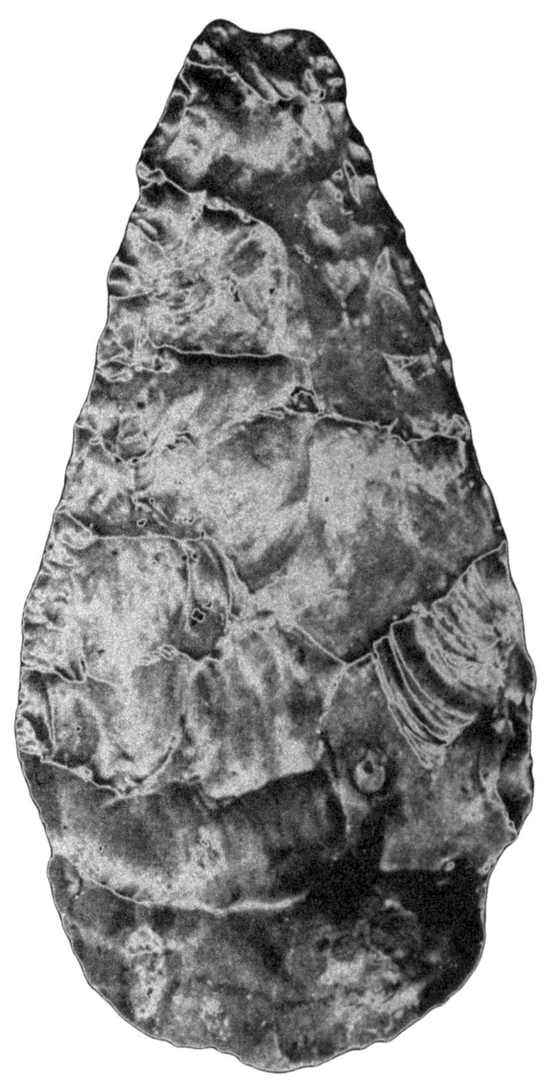

With a few exceptions from the animal kingdom, design is also uniquely human — we can envision something better and create a plan to realize that vision.

When the design profession was still in its infancy — finding its footing between industry and commerce while leaning on architecture and the arts for strategic and philosophical underpinning — the great mid-century architect George Nelson quipped,

"I have never met a designer who was retained to keep things the same as they were."

At Nike, this relentless spirit of design has driven 50 years of innovation dedicated to advancing human potential and creating the future of sport.

ited States Patent Office

977,19
Registered Jan. 22, 197

PRINCIPAL REGISTER
Trademark

Ser. No. 414,177, filed Jan. 31, 1972

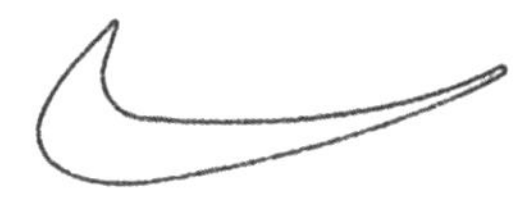

. (Oregon corporation)
. 112th Ave.
n, Oreg. 97005

For: ATHLETIC SHOES WITH SPIKES AND ATH LETIC UNIFORMS FOR USE WITH SUCH SHOE in CLASS 22 (INT. CL. 25).

For: ATHLETIC SHOES WITHOUT SPIKES AN ATHLETIC UNIFORMS FOR USE WITH SUC SHOES, in CLASS 39 (INT. CL. 25).

First use June 18, 1971; in commerce June 18, 197

STERED FOR A TERM OF 20 YEARS FROM January 22, 1974

Attest:

MAY 10 1976

Certified to be a true copy of the registratio issued by the United States Patent & Trade Office, which registration is in full force an

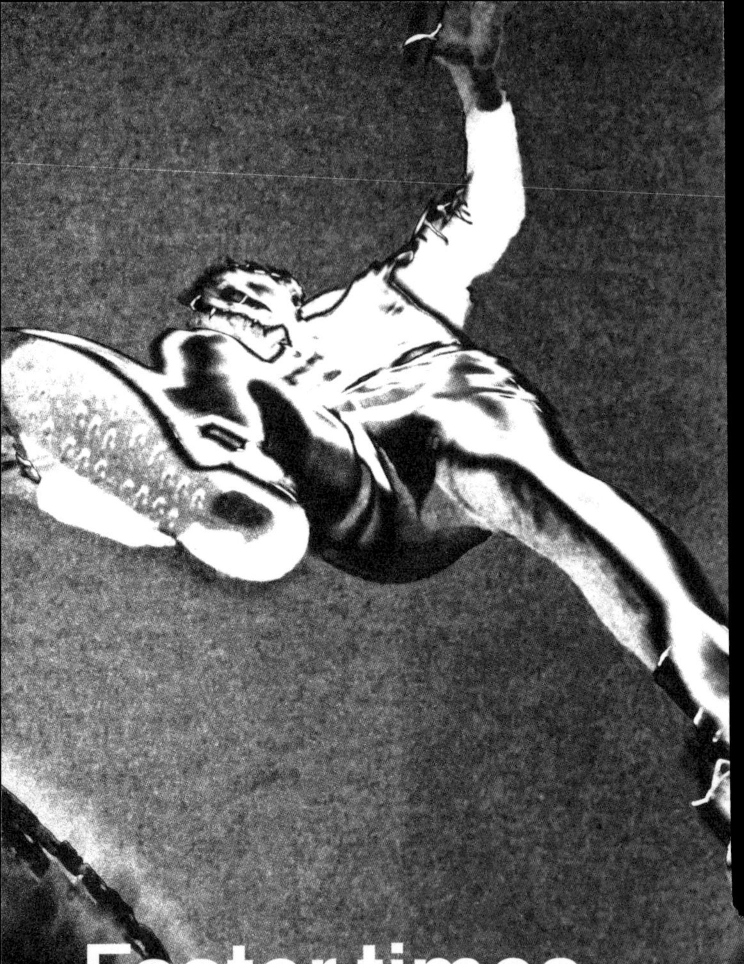

Faster times, longer jumps, tighter cuts, higher scores:

these have all been designed. Fueling this accomplishment has been a process of continuous learning, sometimes through the electric zap of a bold leap forward, but more often through hard-won trial and error.

New Nike designs don't appear out of nowhere. They are the result of decades of accumulated knowledge, athlete feedback, material innovations, sport science, technological breakthroughs, and stylistic decisions. Each successive product charts a new point on a never-ending journey forward, and with that, the direction of the journey (as it stands today) comes a little more into focus.

As you encounter a new design, you might ask, "Who is it for? What's changed and what's remained the same? What got left out? What got revived? What materials are different? Why now?" In the answers to these questions are clues to where the company may be headed next. And if history is any indication, Nike is always headed somewhere new.

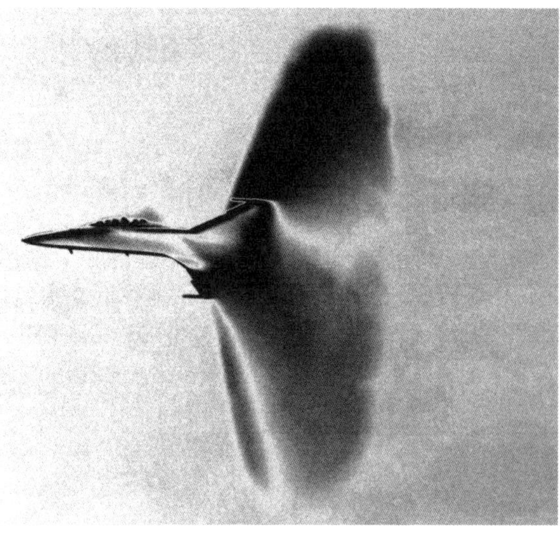

what is it for?
what changed?
what remained the same?
what got left out?
what got revived?

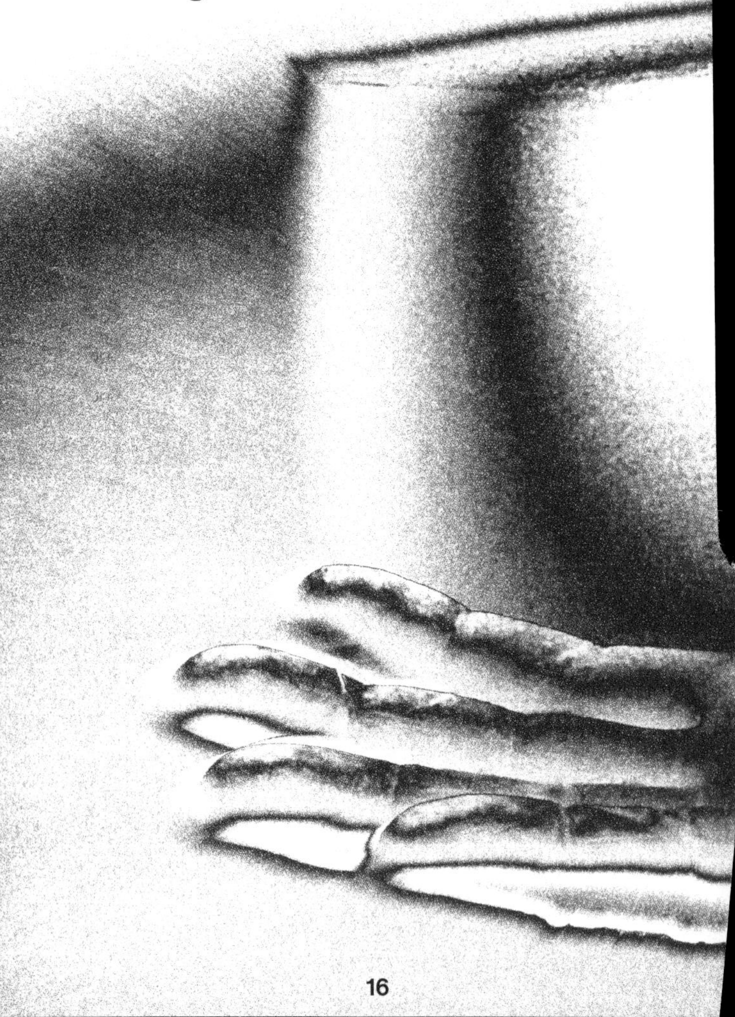

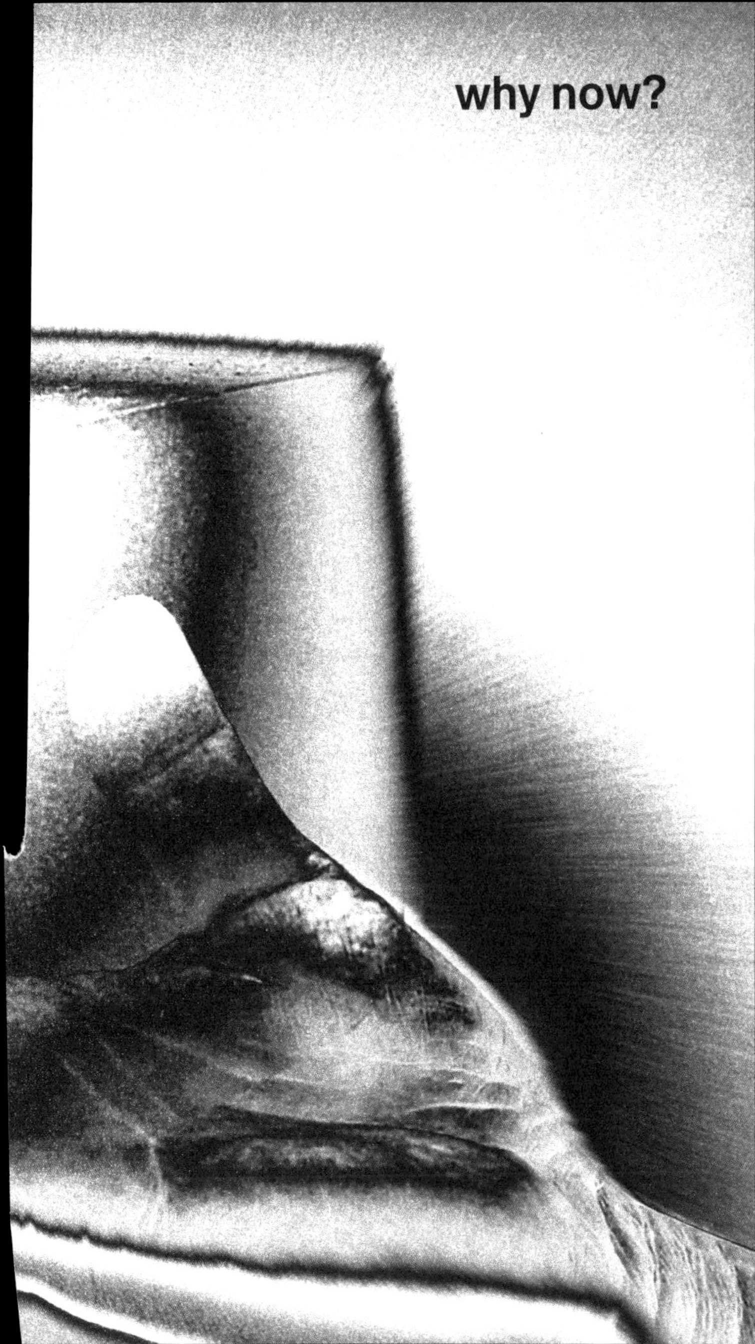
why now?

But to better understand where Nike is going, it helps to understand what lies at the immutable core of everything the company does: the ethos of Bill Bowerman, whose words appear on page one of this book. Bowerman was, of course, the legendary University of Oregon track coach whose relentless drive to bolster athletic performance led to countless experiments in shoe design and eventually to Nike itself. His homespun cycle of tinkering, adjusting, testing, and refining — shaving off a little there for weight, adding a little there for grip — came to define the company's approach to design. If it didn't serve the athlete, if it wasn't vital, it didn't belong. Just as an athlete could continuously improve their performance on the field, a designer could continually improve their output as well. Bowerman's secret? To "always listen to the voice of the athlete.*" It remains the central tenet of Nike design.

And while there is no shortage of Nike athletes passing through the company's unparalleled Sport Research Lab to share their voices, the concept takes on a far greater dimension when you factor in the asterisked addendum:

*If you have a body, you're an athlete.

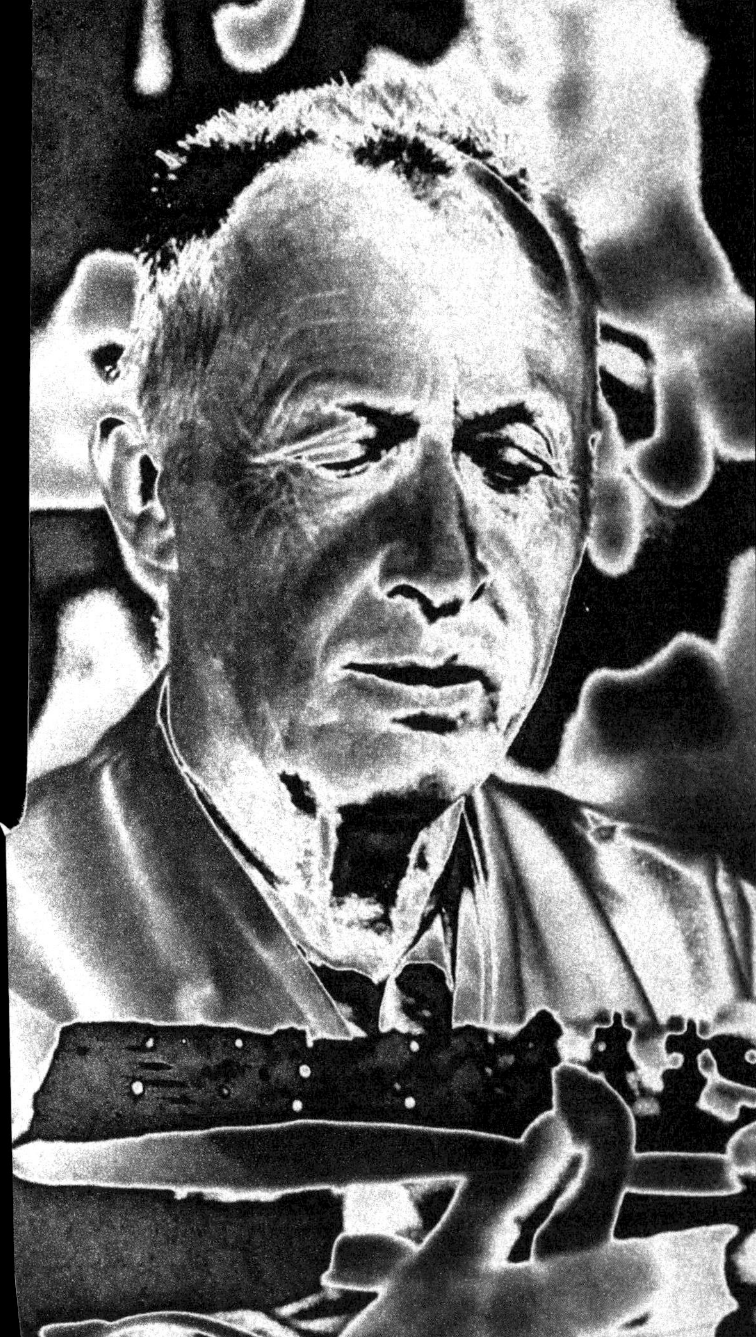

Part of Bowerman's genius was that he didn't just believe in making things better for elite athletes; he thought a more active lifestyle could benefit everyone. (His 1967 book, *Jogging: A Physical Fitness Program for All Ages*, offers ample evidence of this democratic bent.)

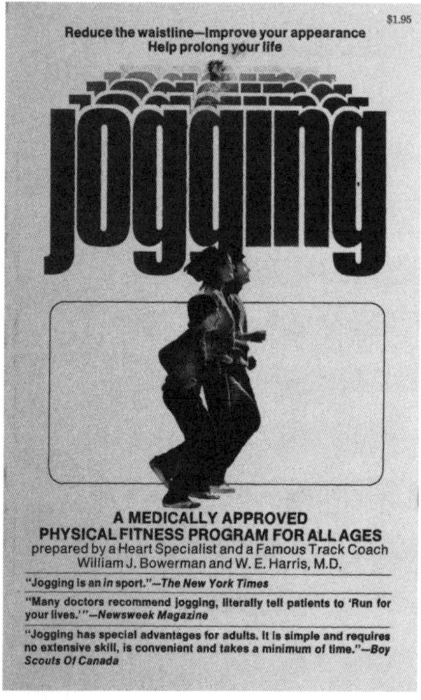

Although Bowerman remains a guiding light, today's Nike is vastly changed. Consider the scale of the company's Beaverton, Oregon, headquarters, the intricate interdependencies of its global supply chain and distribution network, and the quantity and variety of designers under its employ. Nike is now a massive organization with outsize goals, outsize influence, and outsize complexity.

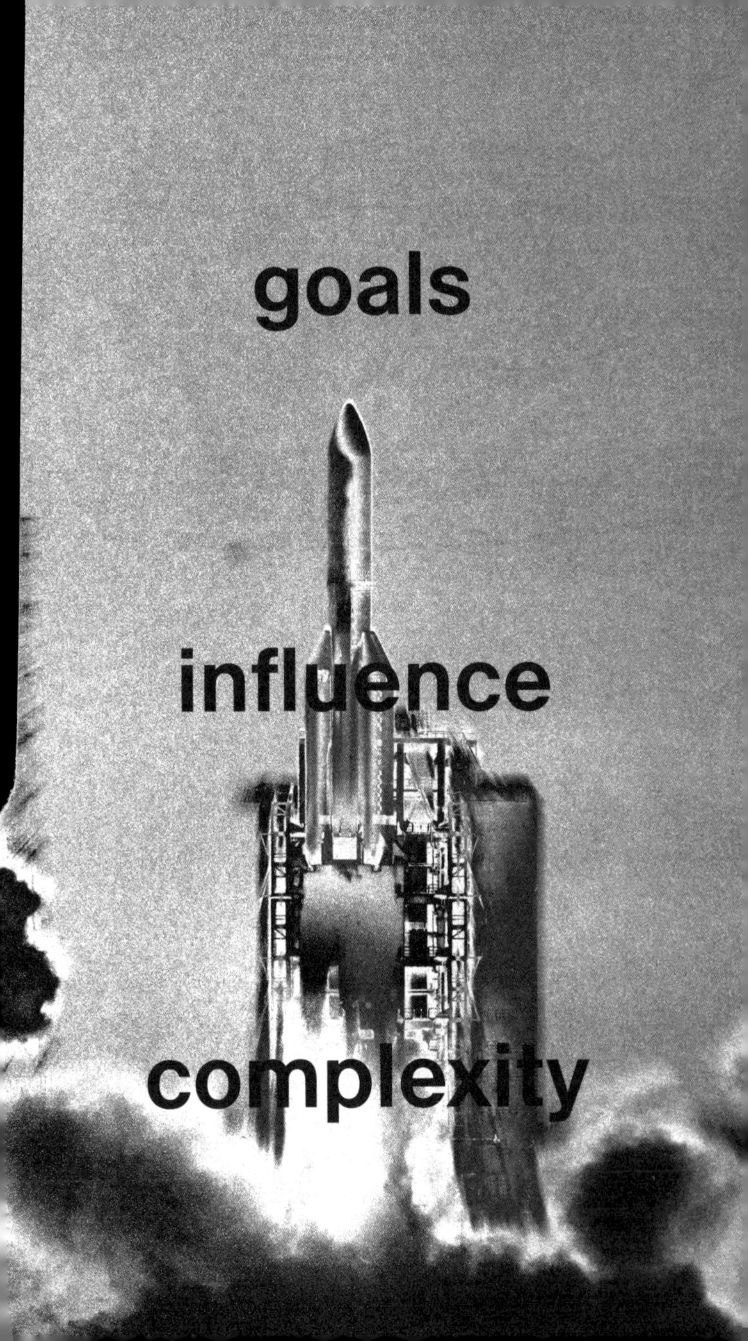

goals

influence

complexity

However, Bowerman's approach and philosophy continue to resonate precisely because they provide an anchor amidst this vast sea of perpetual change. Being rooted in core principles gives the thousands of people who contribute their energy and ideas to Nike a shared foundation from which to operate collectively.

As Nike aims to make everyone with a body a better athlete, it has systematized a framework to consider the fundamental human factors that go into each successful product.

Everybody wants to be protected: safety is a basic human desire. *Everybody wants to belong*: whether it's two or 2,000 people, being part of a community enriches people's lives. *Everybody wants to be informed*: no matter your ability or skill level, athletes benefit from insights and data that contribute to improving performance. *Everybody has a version of better*: setting goals, and harnessing motivation to meet those goals, is spiritually fulfilling and contributes a greater sense of purpose.

When designs help serve these needs,

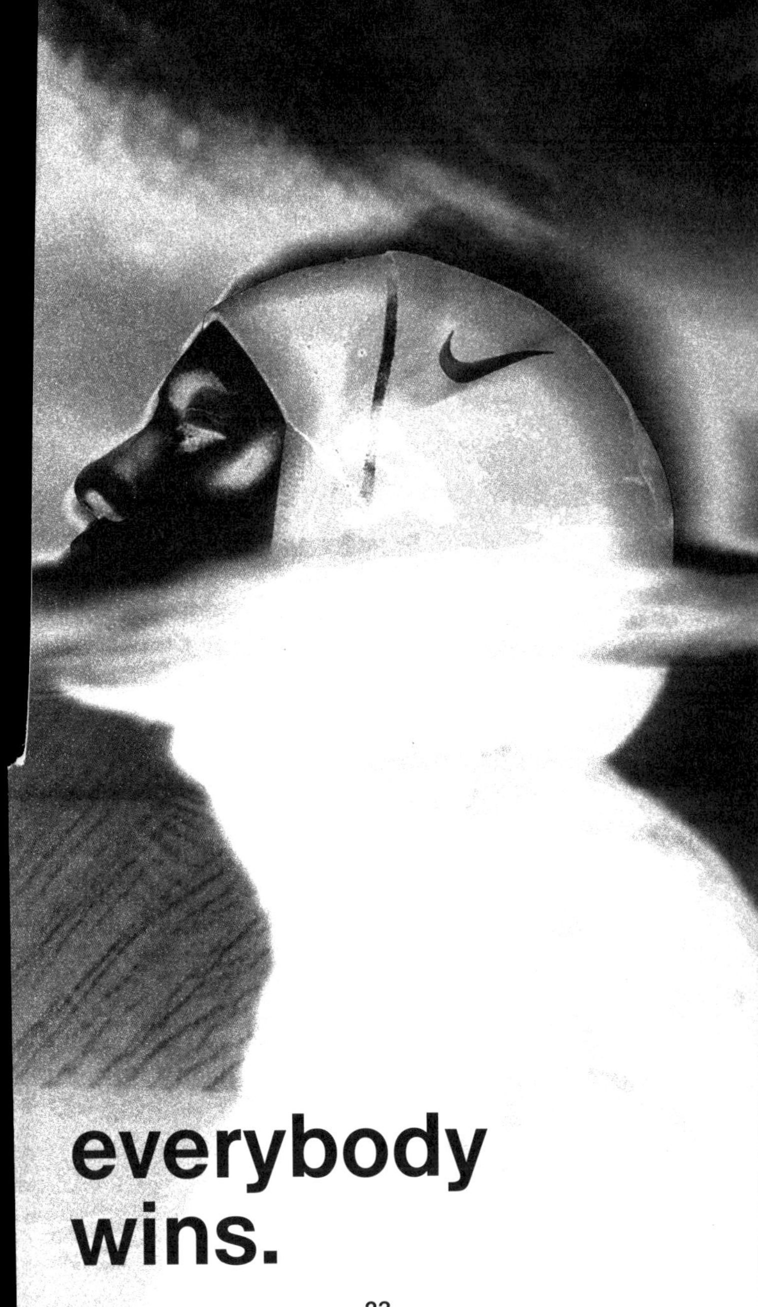
everybody
wins.

By extending this framework in countless directions, Nike has become one of the most recognizable and powerful brands in the world, always at the forefront of culture. Many words have been dedicated to how it got to be that way, but relatively few have been dedicated to where it is heading. There is no crystal ball that will give us all the answers to that question, but there is a language that helps us understand how it will get there.

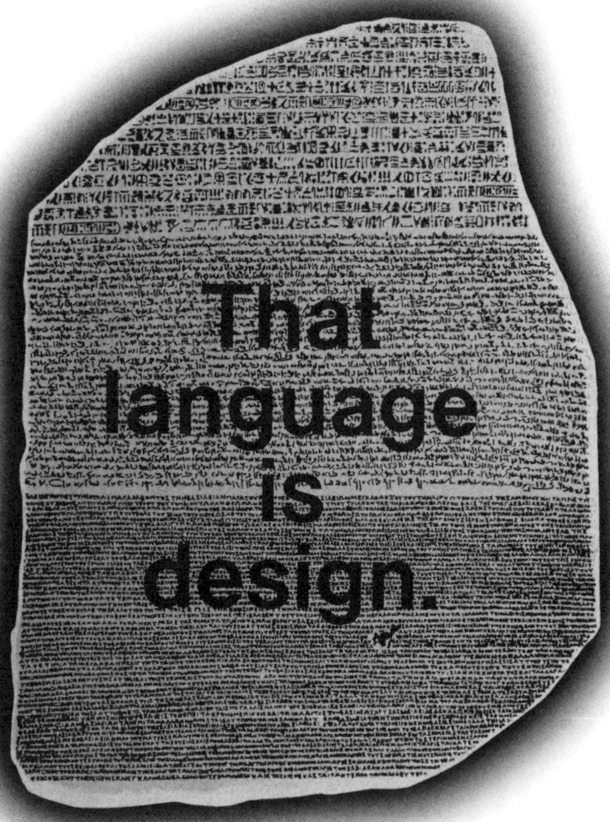

While there are departments and job titles at Nike that contain "design," the most generous definitions of the word don't limit it to certain professions or skills. Design is the most basic of human activities, as old as our species itself. The planning and patterning of any act toward a desired, foreseeable end constitutes a design process. It's how we negotiate our environment, each other, our survival and propagation. Although we may not have considered it in this light, we are all here today, doing what each of us does, because of design. Any attempt to separate it, to put it in its own lane, negates its value as the underlying matrix of life.

And if this is how we consider design writ large, design is no different within the microcosm of Nike. Through one lens, the organization itself has been designed to accomplish its stated goals. Through another, design at Nike is a more specific language and lexicon — encompassing everything from the Swoosh and airbag to Flyknit and the color Volt — that has been developed through contributions from thousands of people who helped get the company to where it is today. As that language evolves, it evolves intentionally — through acts of design.

At Nike, the role of design is to always challenge conventional wisdom, to upend the establishment, to question what has become normal, and to lead to surprising new avenues of discovery. Design shapes a new reality, and that new reality shapes the next round of design.

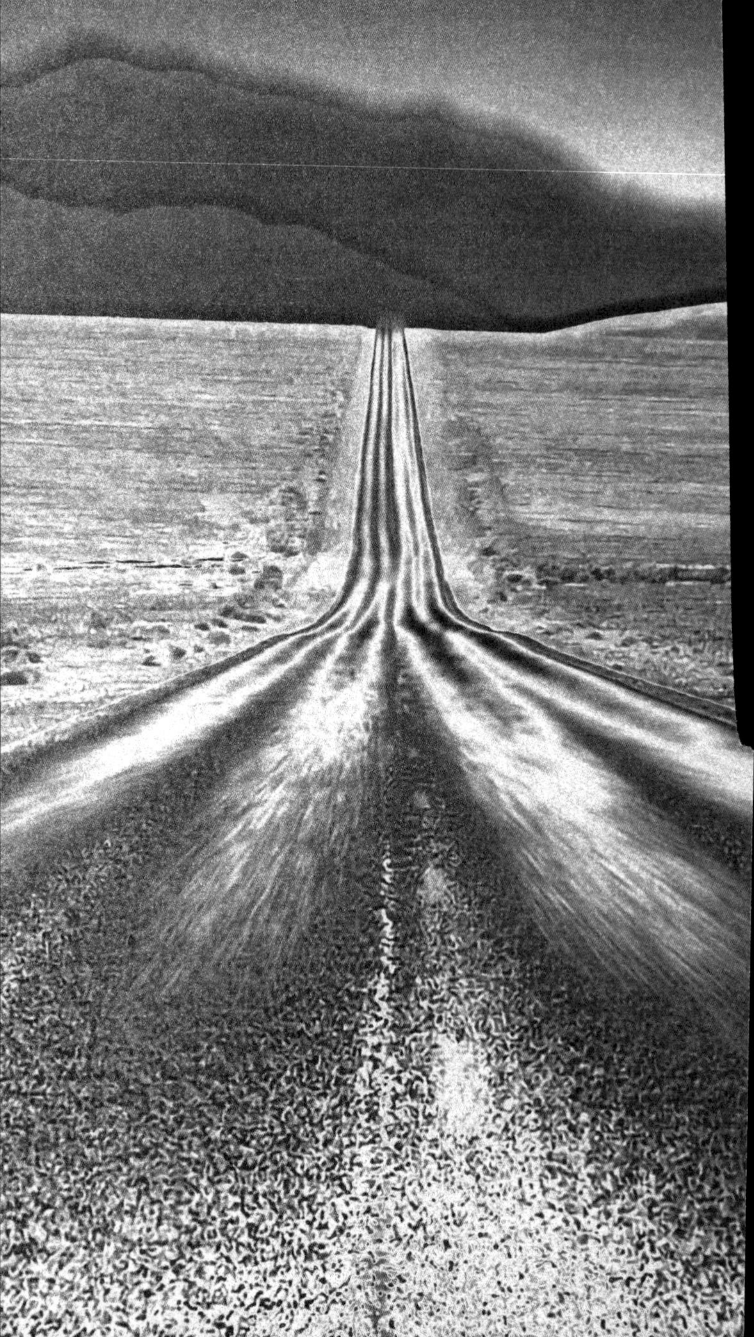

Design isn’t an outcome—

it’s an endless journey, a work in progress.

To that end, at the beginning of 2022, as Nike embarked on its 50th year,

the creators of this book initiated a series of conversations with a diverse range of designers and design-adjacent experts across Nike to probe the current state of the company's work in progress and hypothesize on its trajectory.

Over the subsequent months, as those wide-ranging discussions took us from Web3 and the metaverse to aquaculture and augmentation, larger themes began to emerge out of the dialogue, leading directly to the chapters (and fictional interludes) that follow. While framed as five dynamics transforming design *within* Nike, these themes also surface broader shifts that will reverberate well beyond Beaverton.

If you happen to be reading this 50 years from now, as Nike turns 100, the pages ahead may be laughably inaccurate and demonstrative of the limitations of today's thinking. But there is one certainty: there will be new problems that require new solutions, so the designer's work will never be done.

No Finish Line invites everyone to imagine the infinite possibilities of design — and sport.

No Finish Line draws on 50 years of advancing human potential to move the world forward.

No Finish Line describes Nike's culture of innovation via the athletes, designers, and scientists at its cutting edge.

No Finish Line celebrates design not as an outcome, but as an endless journey.

No Finish Line suggests we can shape a better future by simply daring to create it.

After all, there is no finish line.

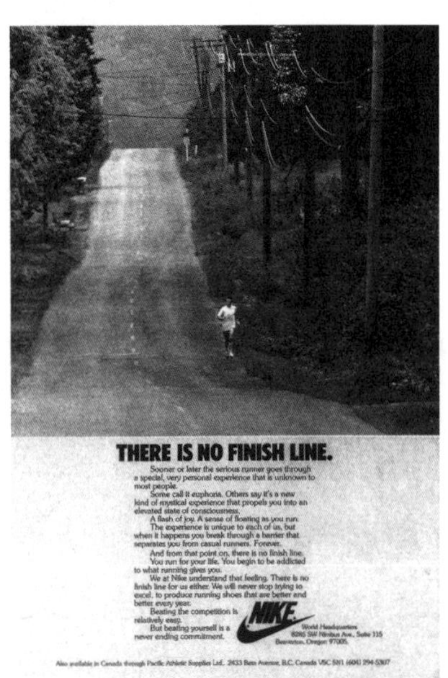

Elite to Everyone

On August 5, 1984, Joan Benoit Samuelson split from the pack in mile three of the first women's Olympic marathon.

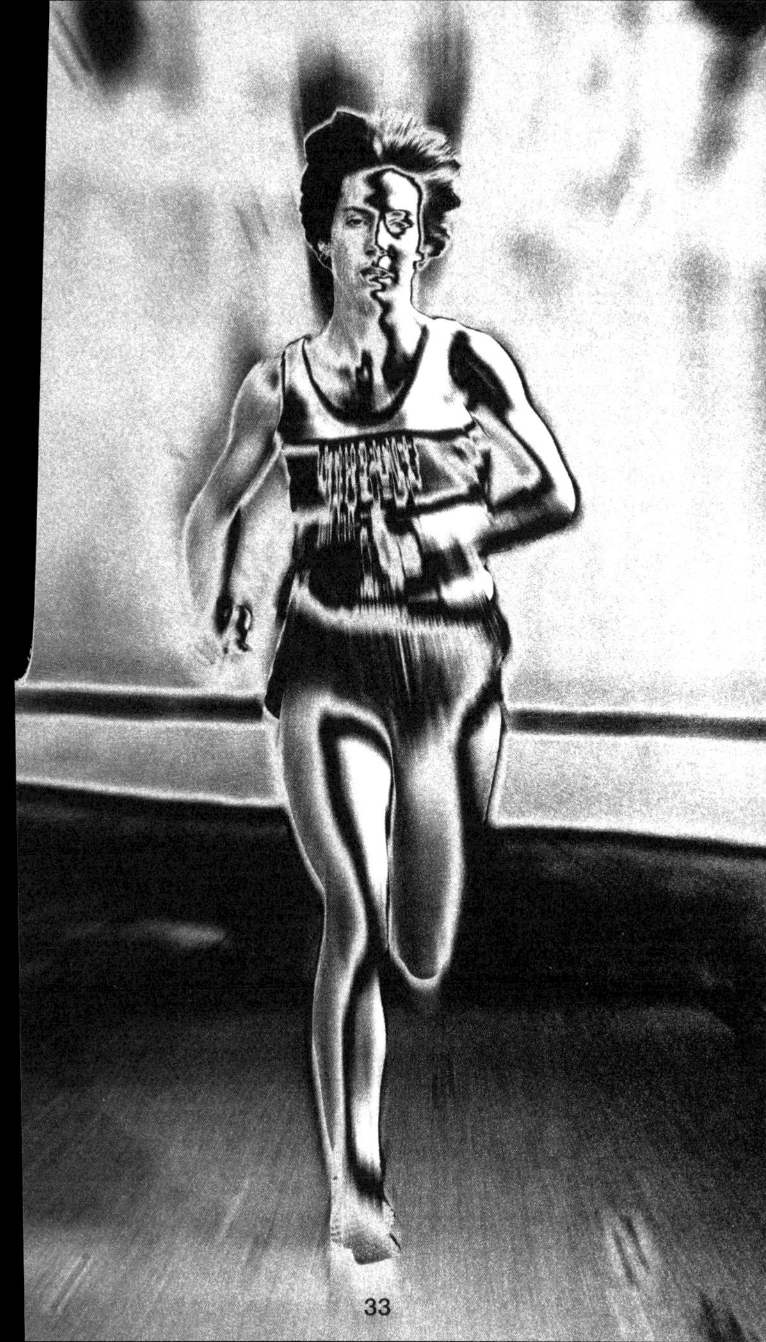

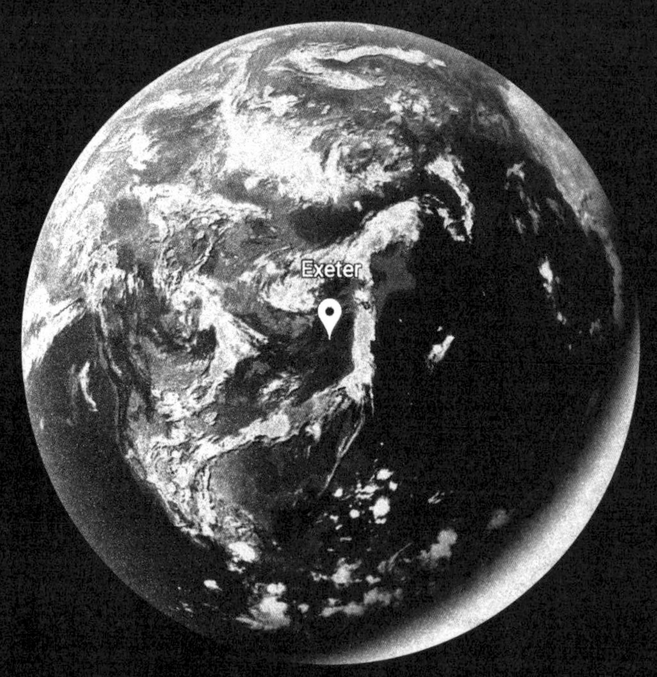
Exeter

She maintained her lead for the duration of the race and, despite the searing Southern California temperatures, recorded a time that would hold as the Olympic record for the next 16 years. Her incredible win was one of the great Olympic performances in history. But more importantly, it helped shatter the world's assumptions about what women athletes were capable of.

While the world may have been taken by surprise, Benoit Samuelson's capabilities were well known to a small team of sport researchers and scientists in Exeter, New Hampshire. The Nike Sport Research Laboratory (NSRL) was established there in 1980 in what could best be described as a glorified shed. The surroundings may have been unremarkable, but the Lab housed some of the most state-of-the-art technology available to study biomechanics, exercise physiology, and functional anatomy—and to help researchers put Nike's product to the test through a range of experiments.

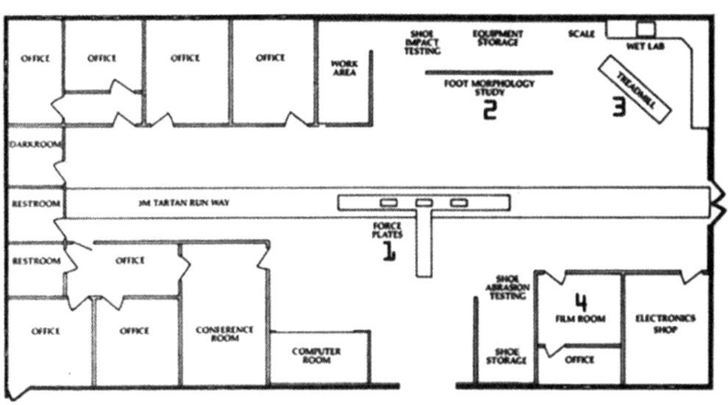

The key ingredient fueling these inquiries and analyses was actual athletes. And not just any athletes, but the world's best — including Benoit Samuelson, who signed on as Nike's second woman athlete after her Boston Marathon win in 1979. At the NSRL, she helped Nike compile data through her own treadmill tests and product feedback. This was part of a mutually beneficial relationship in which Benoit Samuelson's participation helped her better understand what her body was undergoing during a race and how and where she could improve. Her tests and data helped Nike better understand how their products were

serving athletic performance at the highest levels.

NIKE SPORT RESEARCH LABORATORY

The NIKE Sport Research Laboratory, established in Exeter, New Hampshire in September 1980, furthers the development of athletics and athletic shoes by means of studies in biomechanics, exercise physiology and functional anatomy.

1 FORCE PLATES

Force Plates are used to measure ground reaction forces and center of pressure patterns in running or jumping

2 FOOT MORPHOLOGY

The foot morphology study uses a system of mirrors which allows the foot to be viewed and photographed from several angles

3 THE TREADMILL

The treadmill is used to study the oxygen demands of running and as a stationary position for filming the actions of a runner in motion

4 THE FILM ROOM

In the film room gait and foot strike problems are best studied through computer digitation analysis of high-speed photography

2 FOOT MORPHOLOGY STUDY

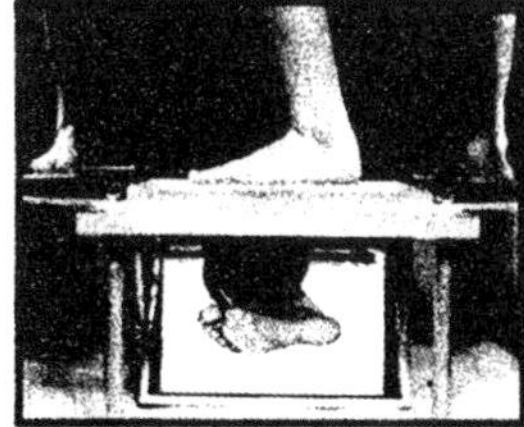

3 THE TREADMILL

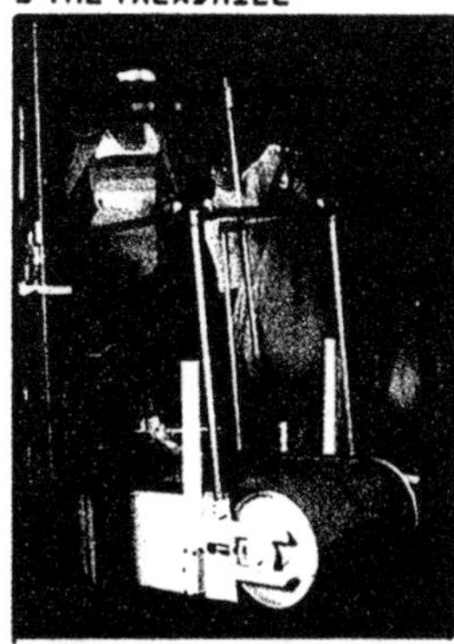

1 FORCE PLATES

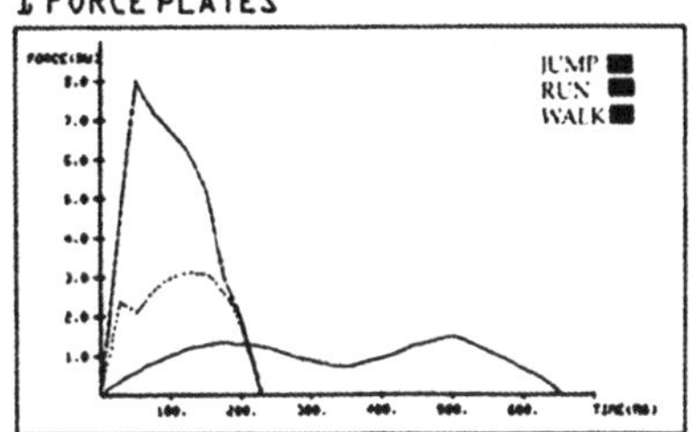

4 IN THE FILM ROOM

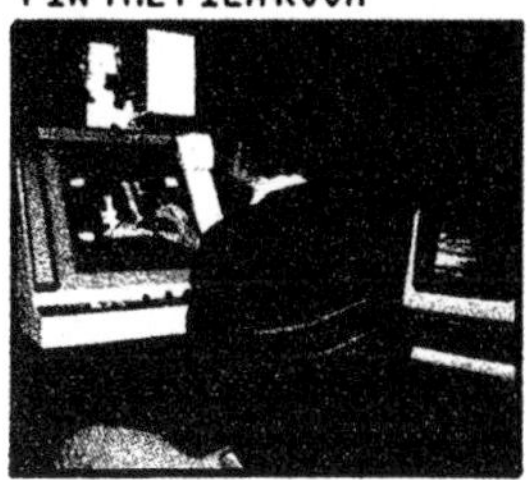

The team's assortment of physical trainers, physiologists, podiatrists, biomechanists, engineers, and data scientists was questioning some of sports' perennial problems—

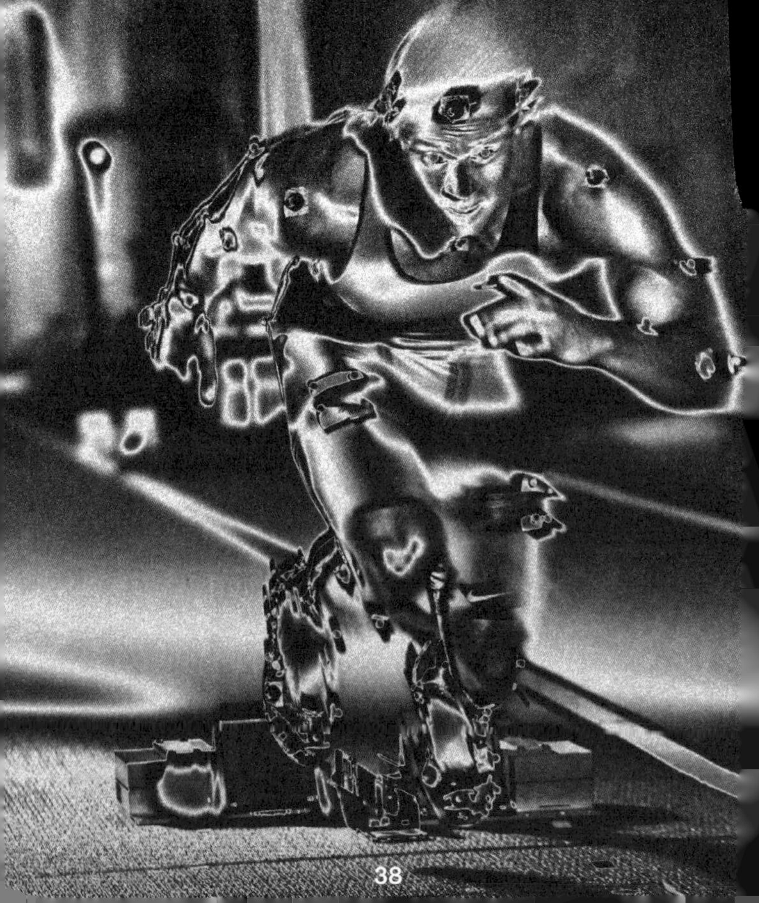

how to run longer, faster; jump higher; and cut quicker — problems that Nike's vastly expanded NSRL still gets after today.

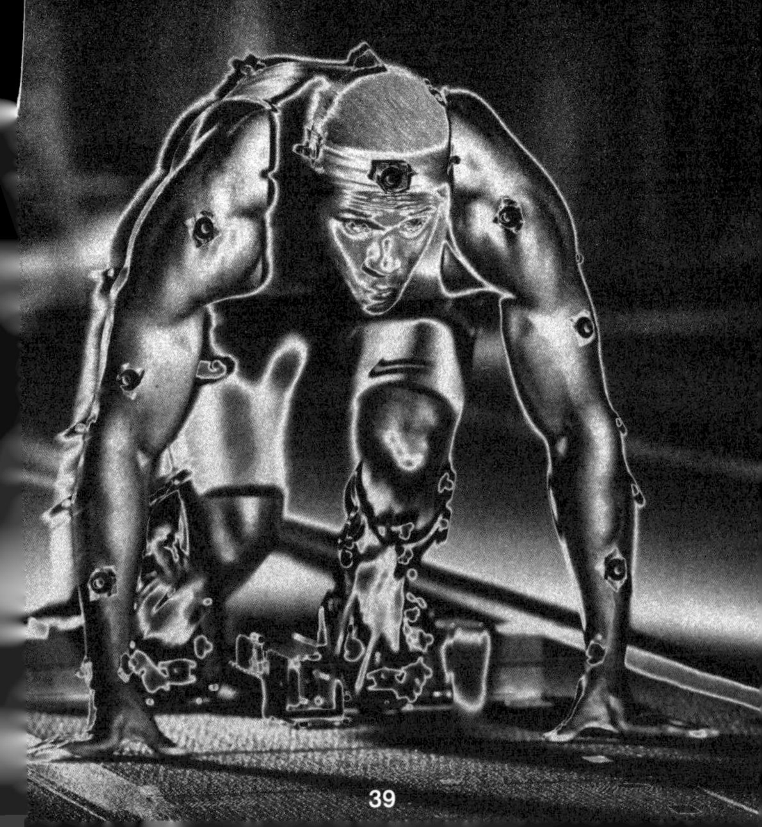

In 2021, Nike debuted the LeBron James Innovation Center, a massive 750,000-square-foot building designed by Olson Kundig that houses the largest and most sophisticated sport research laboratories in the world. Outfitted with all manner of testing equipment, the new facility includes a full-size basketball court lined with motion-capture cameras, a 100-meter straightaway and 200-meter endurance track, half a football field, and four environmental chambers. While the NSRL's basic premise —

to make the athletes of the world better

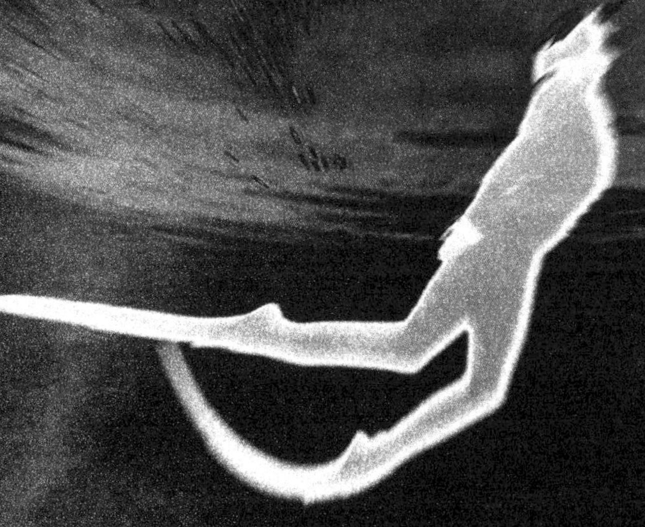

and to make the world better for athletes

— hasn't changed, the expanded space points to the expanded role of research in service of an expanded definition of sport.

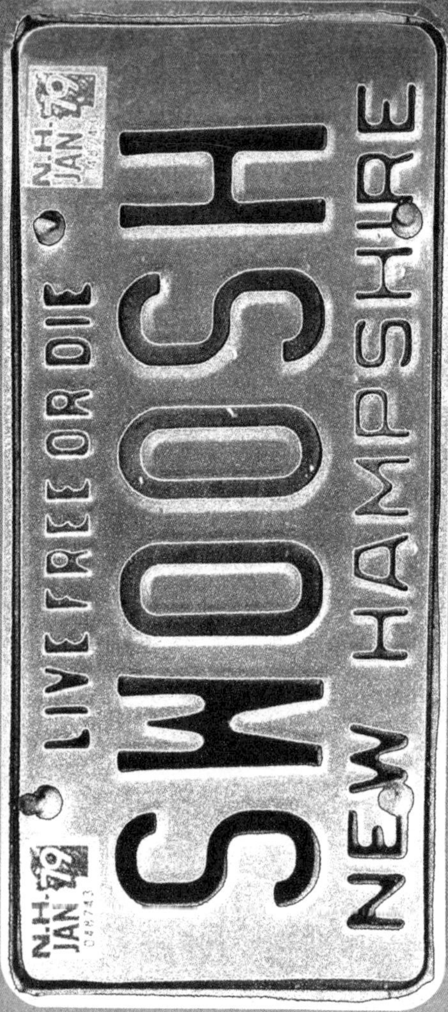

(Bowerman notably viewed Nike as primarily a research company. His license plate reading "NIKE-R," in which the "R" stands for "research," hangs in John Hoke's office today.)

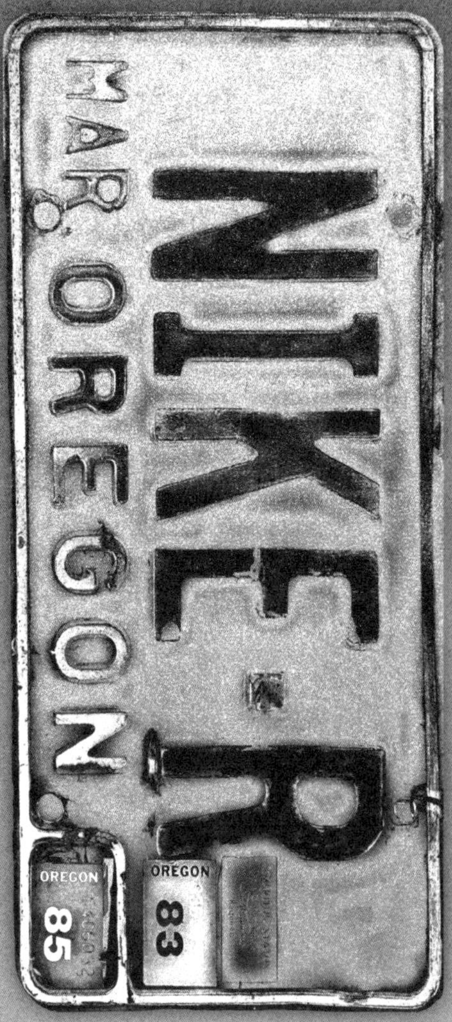

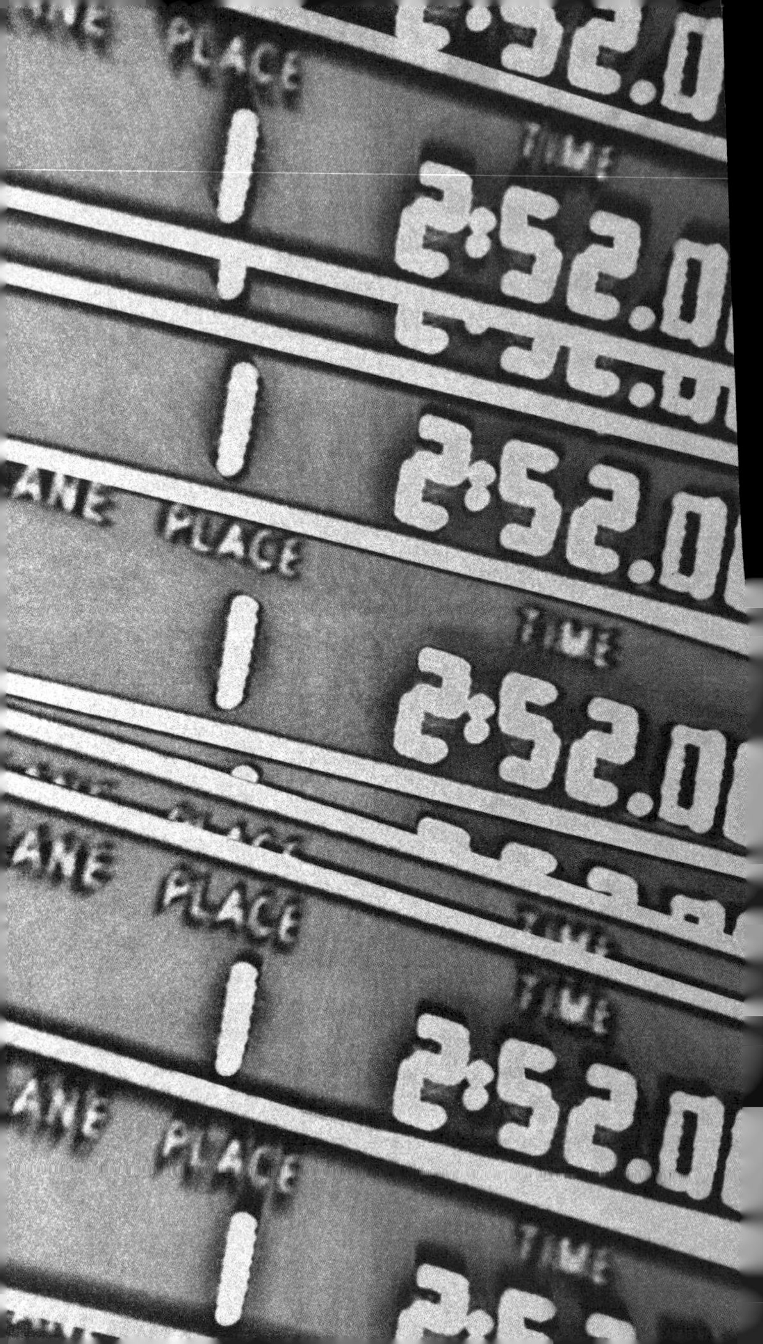
PLACE
1
TIME
2:52.0

At its core, Nike has always been and will always be committed to serving athletes. This began with a focus on running and track and field but soon expanded outward into mainstream competitive sports like basketball, tennis, and global football.

The prevailing strategy has been to attract and work with the brightest talents in each of these areas who drive everything from research and testing to product design and communications. Solve problems for Steve Prefontaine, Michael Jordan, Andre Agassi, or Mia Hamm, and the rest will follow. And while this formula continues to reap rewards, to fulfill its mission of serving all athletes (i.e., everyone), Nike is only getting started.

Already, the company has made significant strides by training its insights and innovation engine on subjects and fields that have been largely unaddressed and underserved: adaptive athletes, pregnant people, modest swimwear, inclusive sizing. With this door cracked open, it's hard to envision a future where it doesn't open wider.

While it may seem odd for one of the world's largest brands to turn its attention to what may outwardly seem like niche populations, the learnings from these investigations expand the vocabulary of Nike design in meaningful ways that often inspire further innovation. As Nike looks to the future, it is laying the groundwork for building relationships with an even broader array of athletes and developing capabilities that will enable a level of personalization and service beyond what it can provide for even the most elite athletes today.

Despite its legendary namesake, ground zero for this expansionary effort is the LeBron James Innovation Center. The NSRL within was designed to welcome not only Nike's most elite athletes, but all athletes. Everyone who passes through the doors undergoes the same baseline testing:

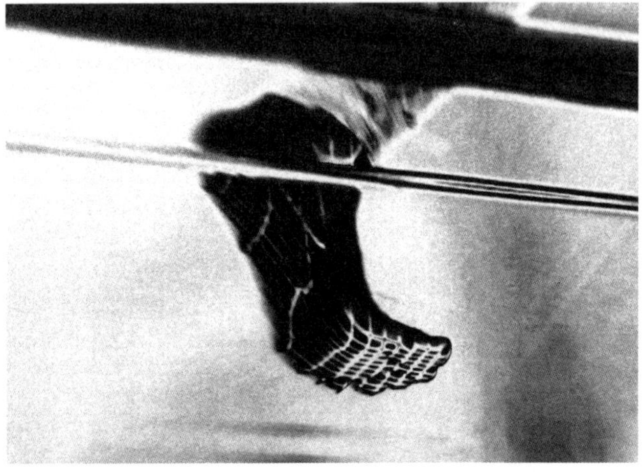

3D body scan, 3D foot scan, underfoot pressure mapping, ankle and toe range-of-motion testing, and countermovement jump analysis. This data serves the individual and helps Nike build a more diverse database of bodies and abilities to fold into their design platforms — all while making sure the data doesn't produce some of the biases that arise when algorithms are trained on certain subsets within a population.

Another objective is to try to make the testing and research process as invisible as possible to the participants. You're not playing a basketball game covered in annoying sensors; you're simply playing a basketball game. This philosophy becomes particularly important to enable research, testing, and feedback around products designed to move with the body.

And while it's critical for Nike to maintain a state-of-the-art facility on its campus, the future of sport research extends well beyond the walls of a single building. Since its inception, Nike has engaged in an extensive wear-testing program, where feedback is gathered and products are measured before and after use in the field. But with a digital layer increasingly underpinning our day-to-day experiences, the ability to collect data from the field will dramatically increase in the coming decades.

With apps like Nike Run Club, the company is already aggregating, from users who opt in, huge amounts of relatively low-level, basic data like heart rate, mileage, frequency of exercise, and so on. The key for the NSRL is to complement the super high-fidelity but low-volume data they get onsite with high-volume but low-fidelity data from the field. With a burgeoning membership program and the possibility of opening satellite NSRL sites around the globe, the goal is to build an ever-more diverse research program that reflects the full range of people and experiences Nike aims to serve.

Today that data from the field may only vaguely point to what's actually happening at its source. As the physical and digital worlds increasingly merge, however, it's clear Nike will be able to manifest progressively more complex and complete pictures of every user.

It's easy to forget that current smartphones, in all their ubiquity, are many times more powerful than the computers that put astronauts on the moon. But still, they exist only as distinct nodes — glowing, handheld interfaces to the vast digital beyond.

Tomorrow's technology will be woven all around us, like the air we breathe or the water we swim in.

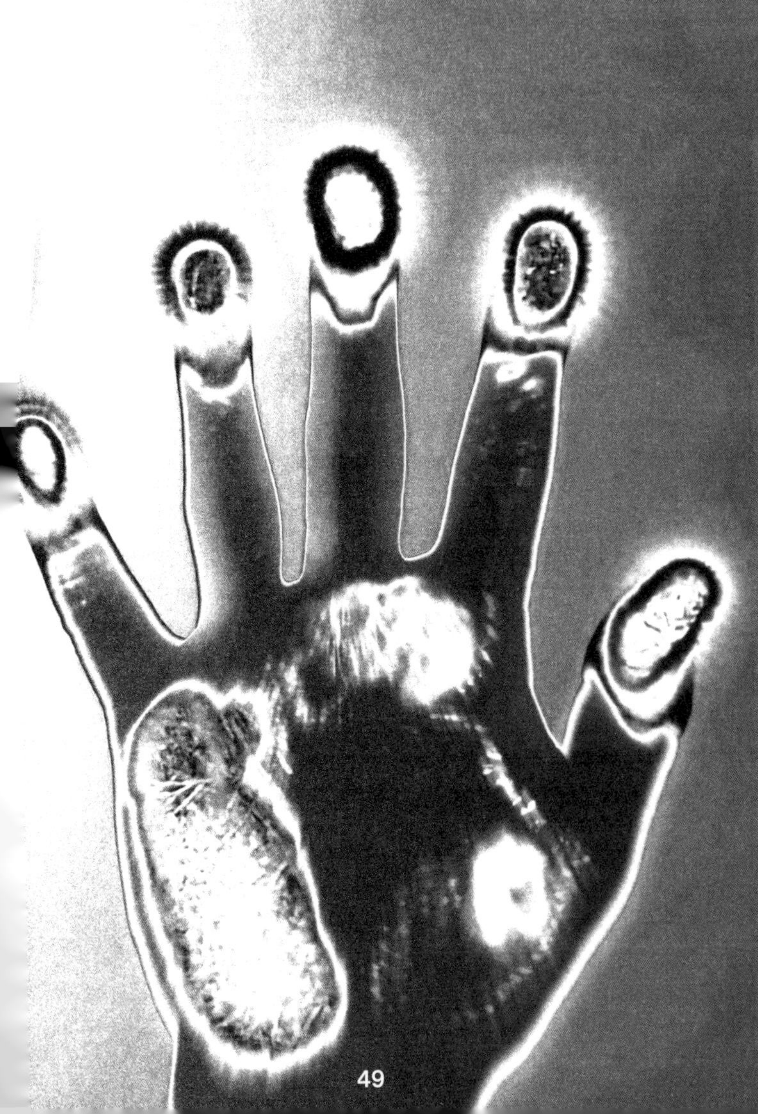

As this new frontier comes to the fore, it presents Nike with the challenge and opportunity to shape the future of sport.

With some of the world's best designers, engineers, developers, and UX/UI experts, Nike's ambition is to create a more human and humane vision of this new, digitally infused world, or metaverse.

Since its earliest days, the company has prized community-building. Even from a physical hardware perspective — shoes and apparel, that is — it's nothing if not a user-experience-driven organization. The transaction has always been in service of a bigger idea, whether that's superior athletic performance or a more expressive realization of your personal style. This same attitude will guide Nike boldly into the metaverse, where everything the company does today, from sport research to storytelling, will take on new dimensions.

Visionaries at the company are already preparing for what this world will become: a place that will enable more people to interact with Nike and each other in the many ways they want to engage. If you're looking for more data about your athletic performance, more coaching, and more motivation, that could be one direction. If you want to meet and hang out with other people who share your interests in sport and well-being, that could be another. If you want to participate in the design process, either with Nike or with other users, that could be yet another. As this new world surpasses our current conception of what's possible (like an immersive, real-life video game), co-creating altogether new forms of sport, competition, and movement could be yet another.

Whatever direction this all takes, the digital marketplaces of the future will fundamentally change the way Nike develops product to meet the demands of its customers. The recent rise (and fall) of NFTs is instructive of the many ways in which digital commodities can exist, create value, provide a ledger of ownership, and be traded and even redeemed for goods in the real world.

It's hardly a stretch to see Nike products within this context, but what is interesting is the fact that those within Nike view these developments as a means to democratize access, opportunity, and even value-creation and ownership. Picture a marketplace for user-generated designs, avatars, or skins where the royalty doesn't go to the biggest name, but to the unknown kid who had a flash of artistic inspiration. Imagine digital products taking on new qualities or dimensions in different corners of the metaverse. When we open a shoebox today, all the innovation is already baked in. Tomorrow that digital product can keep adapting and evolving to offer a different utility or new expressions.

Even as the company moves into purely digital products and experiences, it's the connection to the physical world — or interoperability between the two — that remains critical. The bridge between these worlds is computational design, additive manufacturing, and mass customization. While scaling operations to Nike's level remains challenging from both a technological and an economic standpoint, it's undeniably critical to Nike's ultimate mission of serving *all* athletes.

With computational design, it takes the same amount of time and effort to create a single shape 1,000 times as it does to make 1,000 different shapes. Armed with the right data, a design could be altered to accommodate the specifics of individual bodies, like footbeds that consider their wearer's morphology.

Where that breaks down currently is there's no way to deliver that level of personalization to the product itself; the only variation is in sizing, and even then, because so much manufacturing is still done by hand, not even the same size of the same pair of shoes is going to fit the same, although that's changing.

Even so, the seeds of the future are being planted now. Venture into Nike's Advanced Product Creation Center, and you'll see yarns being knit into uppers and polymers being printed into midsoles. The tools and capabilities are emergent, but the obstacles remain.

As Nike aims to provide each of us with more personalized products, whether to meet physical demands or aesthetic whims, it will take connecting the dots from one end of the product-creation cycle to the other. That means developing the ability to collect and input unique data from each individual user, feeding that into a computational design platform that can process the variations into customized product, and then outputting and delivering that product through state-of-the-art manufacturing techniques that don't rely on expensive tooling, cut yardage, and onerous handiwork.

If the last 50 years at Nike were about deriving insights from the biomechanics and exercise physiology of the world's best athletes and designing those insights into purposeful and desirable products for everyone,

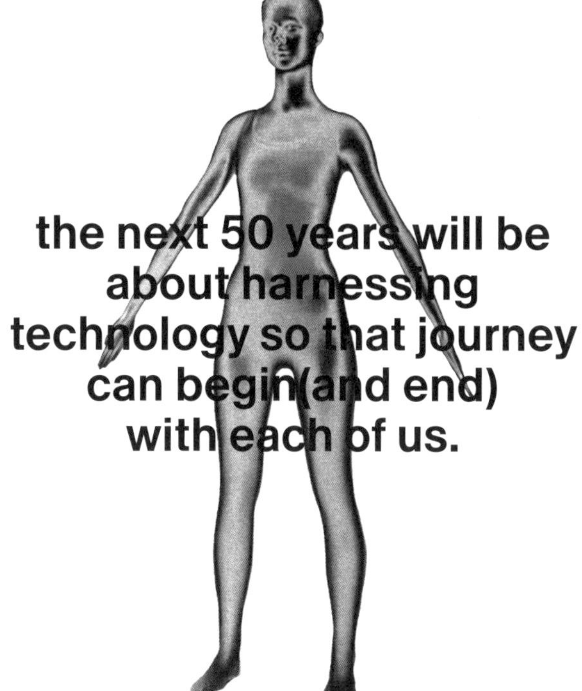

the next 50 years will be about harnessing technology so that journey can begin (and end) with each of us.

That doesn't necessarily mean the future will be driven by machines. Rather, it should entail a turn toward the most deeply empathetic and human design processes Nike has ever undertaken. We all know we're so much more than the sizing letters on a tag or numbers on the side of a shoebox — and Nike does too.

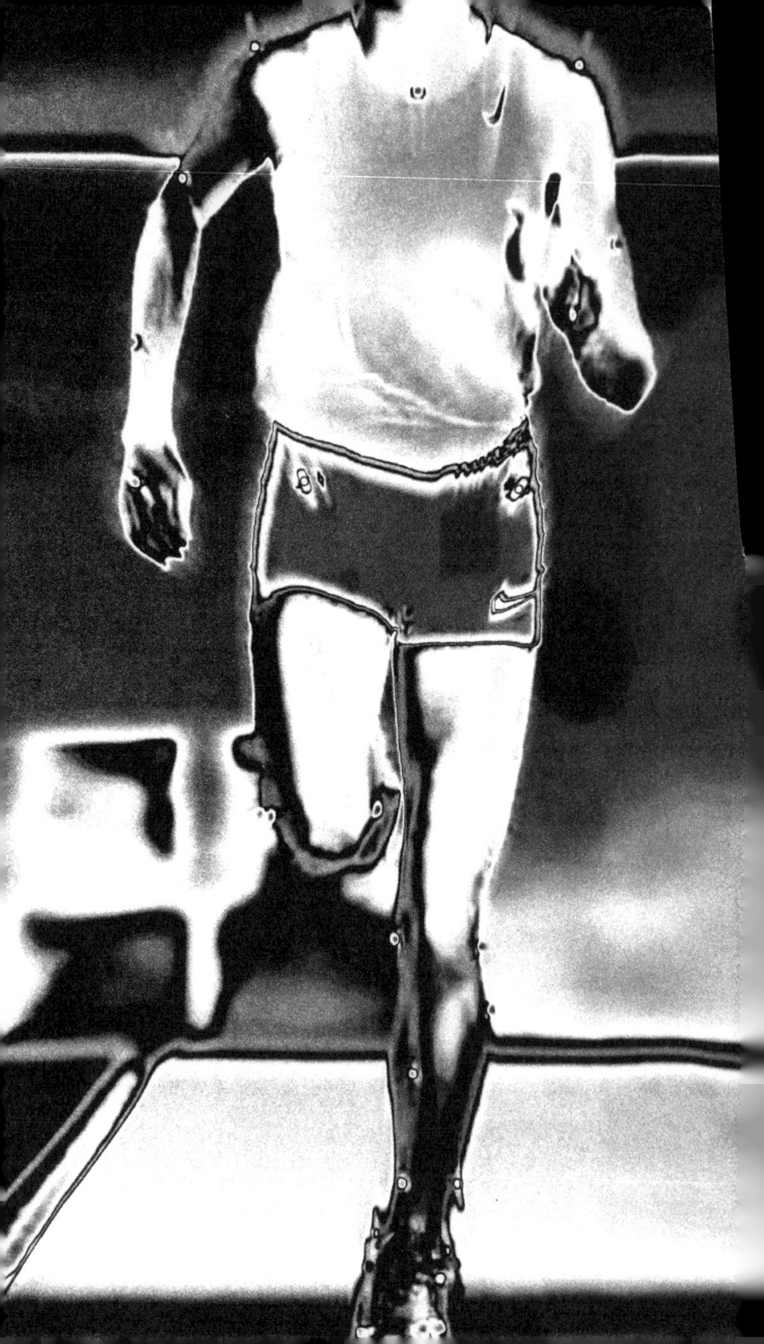

The products once labeled “engineered to the exact specifications of championship athletes”

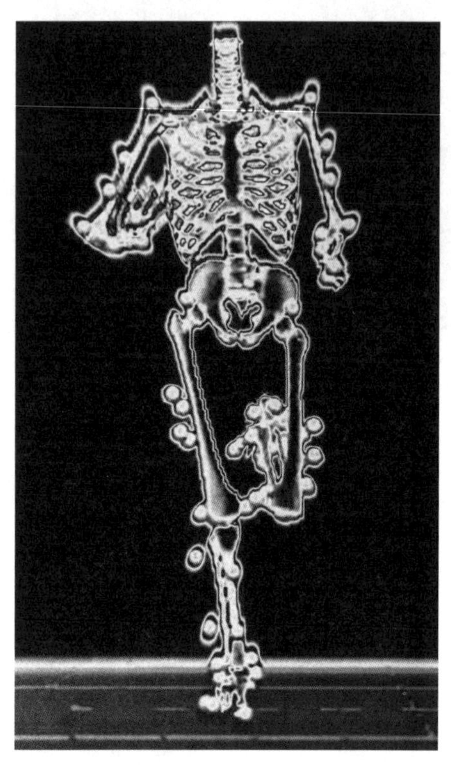

may soon say “engineered to the exact specifications of you.”

Offworld Games

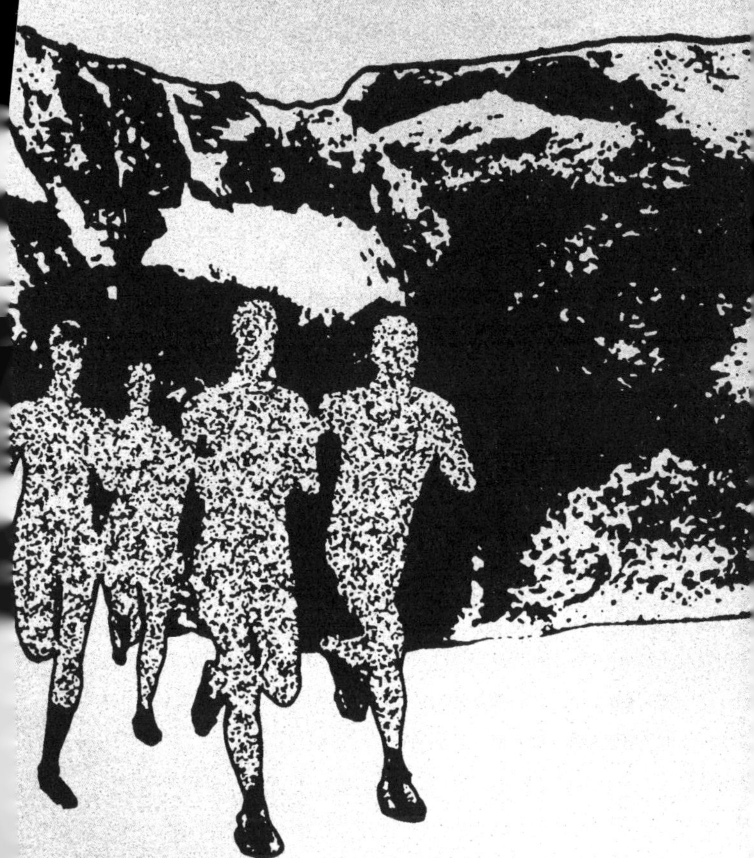

Everyone on the station was a fan — the whole crew. The idea that Hari — *the* Hari — was actually there that day still seemed hard to believe. He had been a dominant force in space games for the past five years, but none of Nike's offworld staff — inspired by him, in awe of his tightly coiled physical intensity and his strange grace — had ever met him in person.

Raised on the playgrounds of Cape Town, Hari was now received like a planetary superstar. (Although, his agent once joked, surely that should be *extra*planetary.) After all, he did most of his stunts hundreds of miles off the Earth's surface. Photos of him grinning through his shatterproof visor made from glass crystals grown on reefs, with Antarctica or the Great Lakes looming below, now graced websites and walls in almost every bedroom on Earth. He was a global inspiration.

As he bobbed past them all in zero gravity, signing autographs here and there, cracking jokes, the crew realized what it felt like to be in one of his famous images: the huge cathedral-like windows all around them showed Australia, the Pacific, South America, and the Atlantic Coast turning past far below.

Nike spacewear had become the gear of choice for offworld athletes and travelers both. Ultrathin insulating fabrics tested in Nike's Shanghai deep-cold facility were more than a decade ahead of any competitor's, and abrasion-proof ceramic coatings for elbows, shoulders, and knees, first fired and tested in the company's desert lab near Nairobi, were ideal for the knocks and tumbles that inevitably hit anyone working — and competing — in space.

For his trip to Nike's offworld facility, Hari had been loaned the newest version of their spacewear gear, milled here among the satellites and stars on advanced zero-gravity looms. Metallic fibers and thread-based sensors helped power his arms and legs in the absence of gravity, so much so it no longer felt like he was even in space.

But it wasn't just the gear that interested him on this visit. It was also the opportunity to participate in the sports themselves. He had almost single-handedly invented the offworld athletic events that many earthbound athletes now dreamed of competing in. Combining skills from gymnastics, climbing, wrestling, and martial arts, the games were calibrated for a body unshackled by gravity.

His enthusiasm, his sheer joy at experiencing space, had inspired a call for the world's first Offworld Games. After years of planning, they would be held next year here, in Nike's flagship orbital facility, a structure circling the Earth several miles higher than the old International Space Station. Much of its huge interior was devoted to this, and the team spent the next few hours sharing ideas for future obstacles and challenges.

Hari convinced one of the ship's maintenance staff to give one of the obstacles a shot along with him. She agreed, excited at first, then nervous. Could she really do it? Offworld athletes moved with such balletic intensity; she didn't even like to exercise. Being forced to turn completely upside down, multiple times, in various contortions, was the least strange part of it, she realized. What is upside down, anyway, when you're in space? It was the focus on different parameters that surprised her, like surface texture and friction, and the use of specific types of fabric to hook onto or slide across barriers and objects.

Her first efforts were comically uncoordinated, even embarrassing, but Hari offered patient instructions, reminding her that entirely different parts of an athlete's body are activated by offworld activities. It was all core and abdominal contraction as she learned to tumble through space, desperately trying to reset her balance with the throw of an arm or a kicked leg. Hari needed no warm-up, of course; the whole crew marveled as he rolled and grappled across obstacles as if he had been born a thousand miles above the world.

As they orbited back around the planet again, she managed to nail one of the moves. She could curl up and explode, propelling herself from one platform to another, bumping her elbows and knees along the way, of course, but she pulled it off. It made her feel like a kid again.

Performance to Promise

Dating all the way back to the ancient world, sport has been represented by public displays of strength, agonistic values, and heroic achievement. Even today, we use physical prowess, technical ability, and statistical ranking as the benchmarks of athletic accomplishment. When the psychological dimension is allowed into the picture, it largely follows the same tropes and storylines. Winners, we are told, possess superhuman amounts of grit, determination, and drive. Perfectly normal emotions such as self-doubt, fatigue, or frustration are typically framed as weaknesses to be eradicated, vulnerabilities for opponents to pry apart.

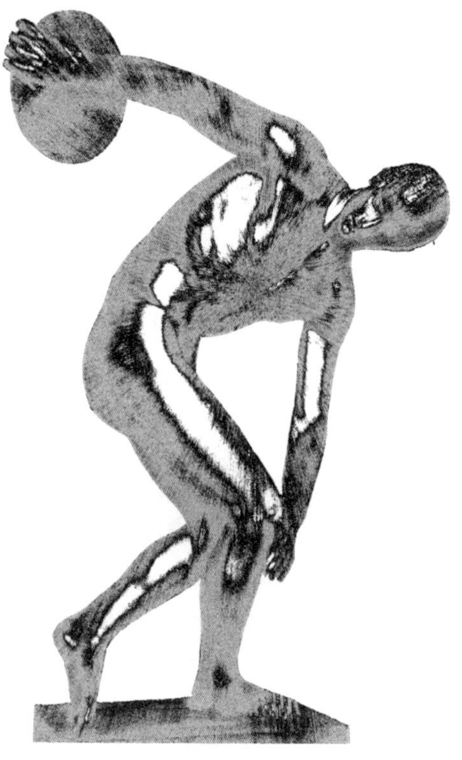

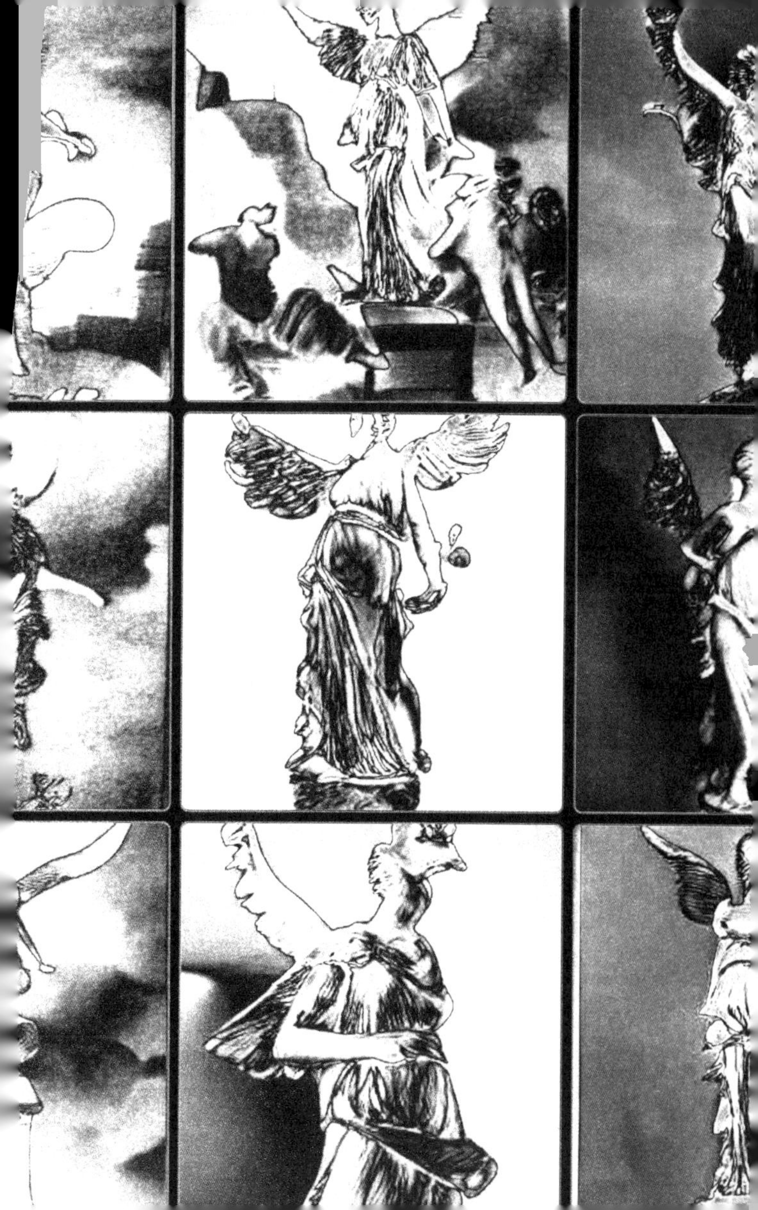

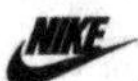

Sooner or later, you start taking yourself seriously. You know when you need a break. You know when you need a rest. You know what to get worked up about, and what to get rid of.

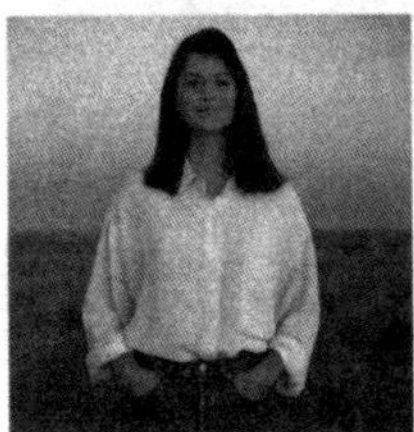

And you know when it's time to take care of yourself, for yourself. To do something that makes you stronger, faster, more complete. Because you know it's never too late to have a life. And never too late to change one.

Just do it.

But the reality is even the greatest athletes on the planet are just human beings, with all our foibles and idiosyncrasies. No one completely exits their mental state when they step onto the playing field.

Acknowledging and harnessing the psychological dimension of sport is increasingly seen as a key driver for enabling excellence in other aspects of play and, more broadly, life.

As Nike contemplates the future, it's not only concentrating its sport research, design, and innovation capabilities onto this largely untapped arena, it's also shifting toward understanding physical fitness within a more holistic model of general well-being.

For its first 40 years, Nike set the gold standard for "below the neck" sport science, focusing its research efforts on physiology, biomechanics, kinesiology, footwear, and apparel. This tracks with the company's original focus on running and elite athletes. If you prove that something's going to help you run faster, jump higher, or cut better, people chiefly concerned with shaving milliseconds off their pace are going to give it a go. But when you start to address the other end of the spectrum, what Nike dubs the "asterisk athlete" (aka everyone), perception and aesthetics play a far bigger role.

asterisk athlete

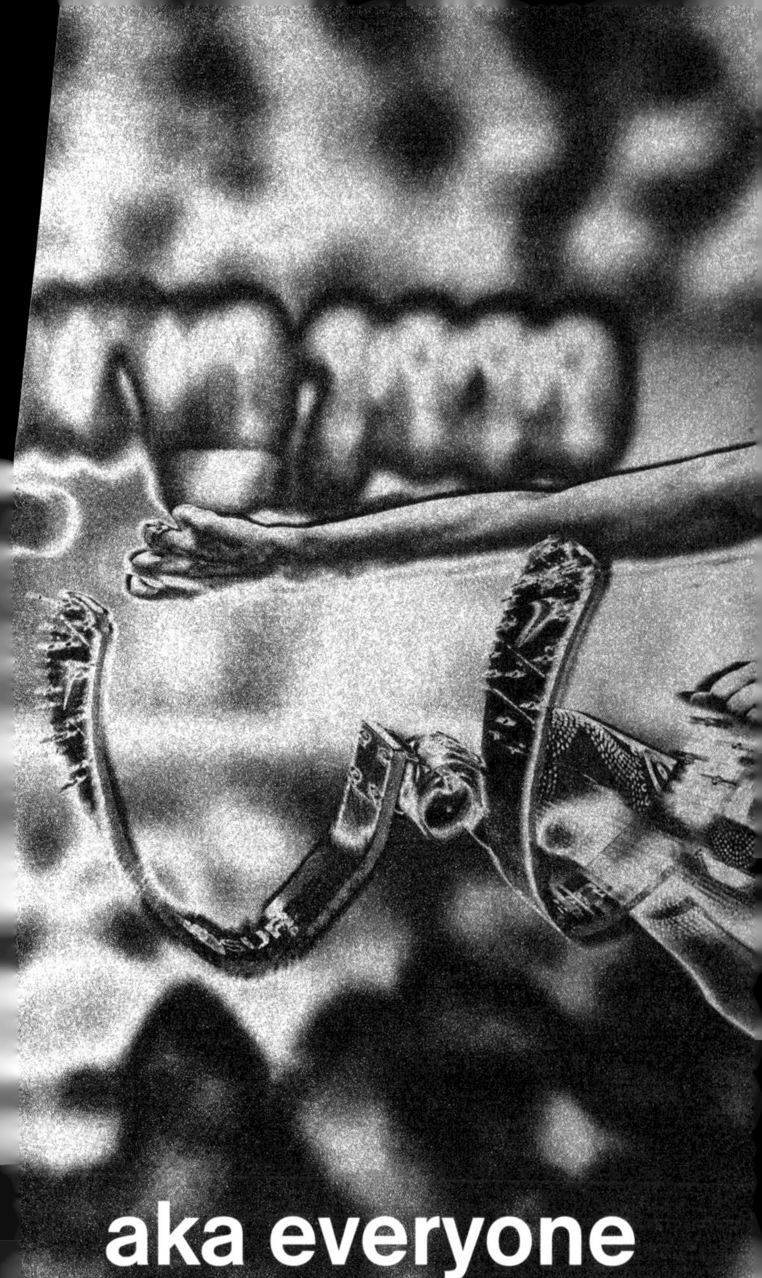

aka everyone

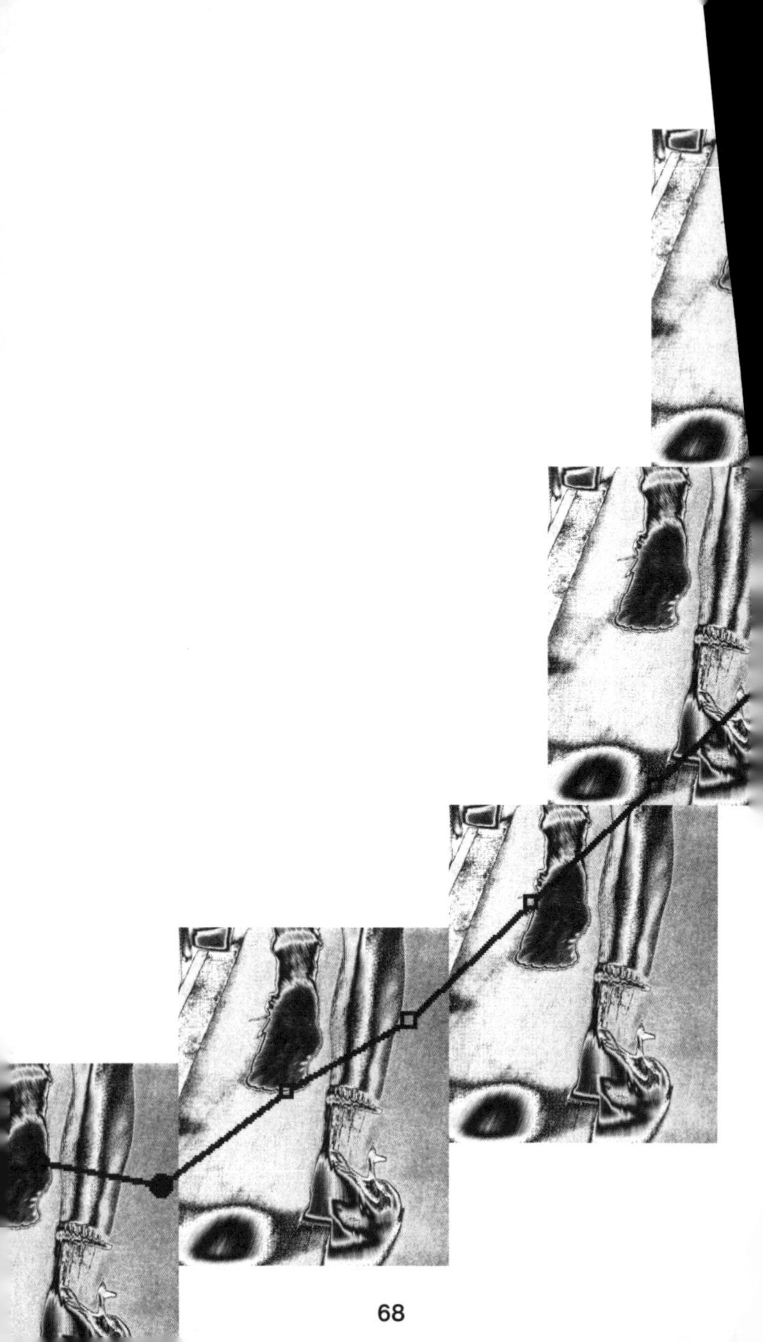

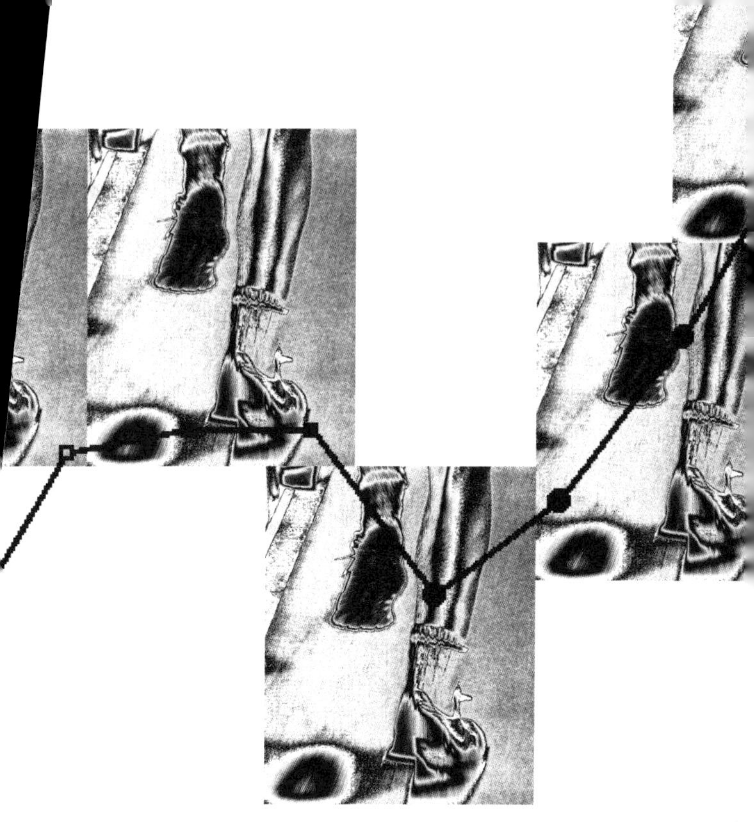

For instance, Nike's researchers and designers have found that with casual runners, the biggest thing to address — somewhat unintuitively — is slowing the foot down and dampening the slapping motion that happens when amateurs (whose foot strikes are not as coordinated as those who have practiced for thousands of hours) break into a full stride. Why? Because the slapping results in soreness, and the soreness turns the runner off from getting back at it for another go.

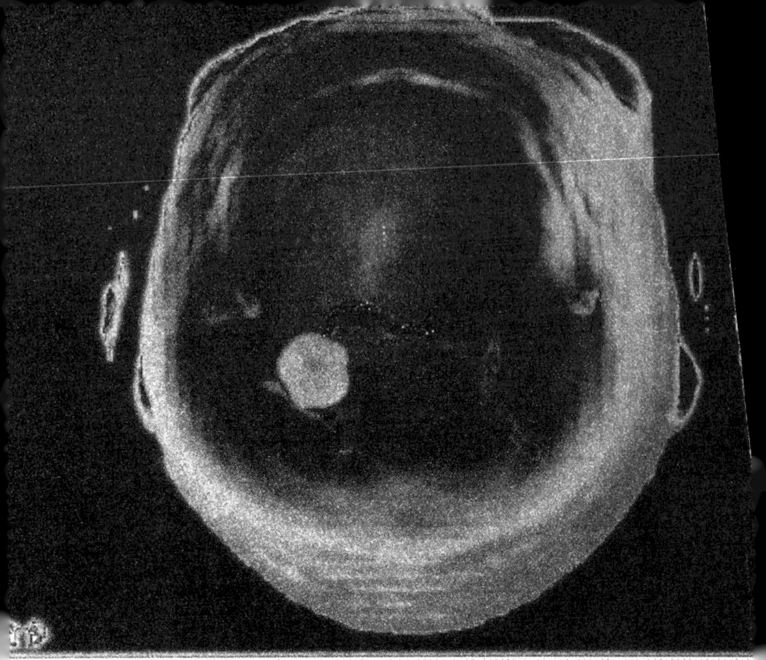

It turns out that even great footwear, when applied poorly, can hinder an athlete's journey. Although this is still just a nascent practice, adjusting for these perceptual cues and incorporating these insights into the design process is starting the company down a path of closing the loop between

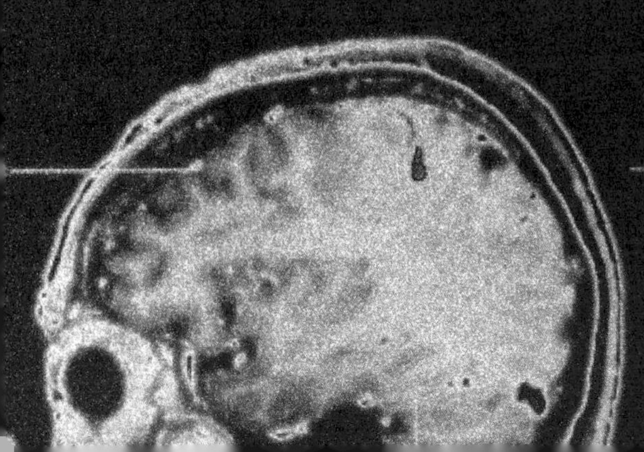

Nike products
and services,

human
psychology and
neuroscience,

and athlete
motivation.

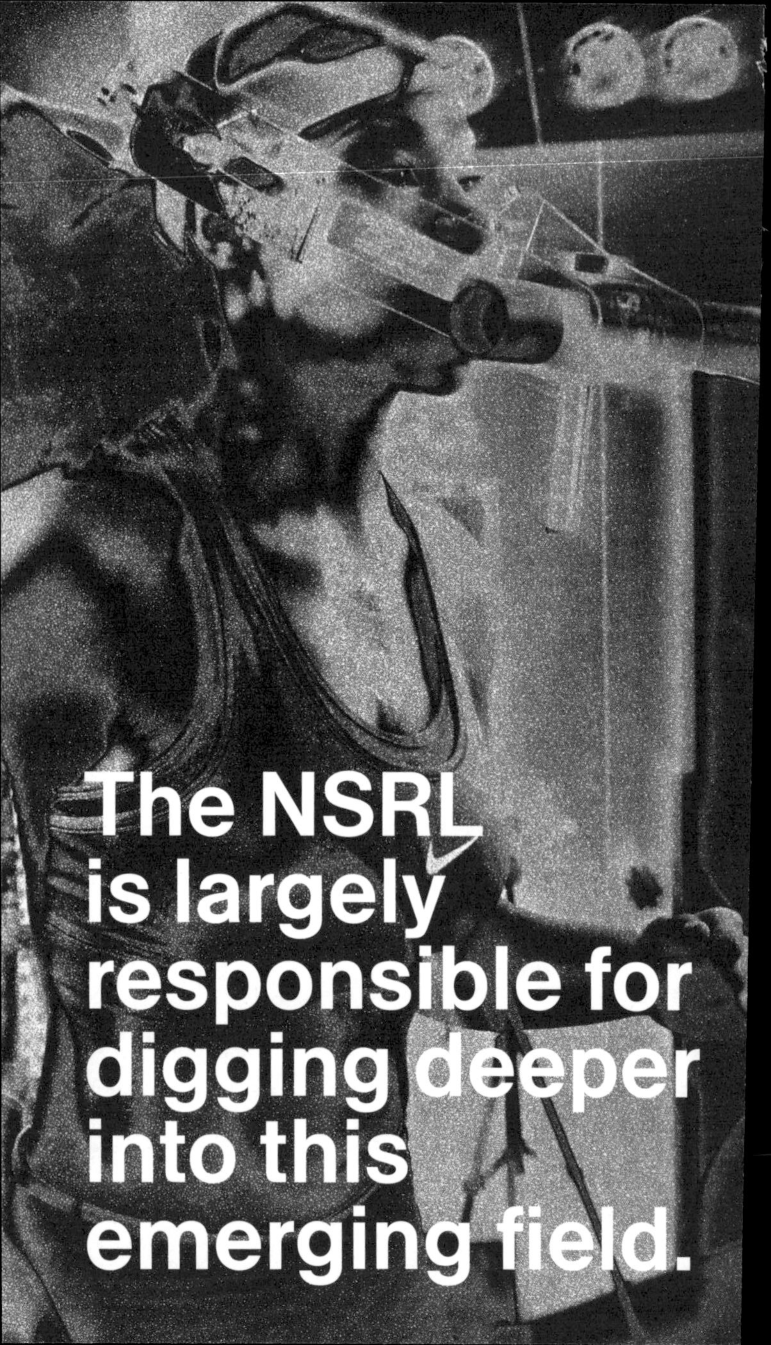

The NSRL is largely responsible for digging deeper into this emerging field.

While every athlete who has ever passed through the lab has established a physical baseline, researchers now also record a cognitive baseline. Developed with behavioral economists and psychology experts, the tests are designed to help Nike better understand your feelings related to your physical state and the goals you're trying to achieve, with the aim of developing cues and recommendations for how best to keep you moving along that path.

New data sets are helping lead the NSRL to entirely new insights from which to design and innovate. As one example, researchers are digging into the psychology of behavior modification, gamification, and nudge theory, along with functional magnetic resonance imaging of the human brain as it responds to different stimuli or types of movement. While the company has rallied around the mantra "make sport a daily habit" for some time, this effort marks the first attempt to really get under the hood and understand how and why that means something entirely different for each of us.

And even though there's still a lot to uncover in the lab, there's even more to do to build a functioning feedback cycle with athletes out in the world. While tech giants are busy collecting all kinds of information about our online habits, a very narrow window of that data gets applied in ways that are actually beneficial to users.

Nike, on the other hand, doesn't want people to exercise as much as possible, but rather, at the level that's right for them and in a way that makes them feel as good as possible as they progress toward their goals. Drawing on data already collected from participating users of their Nike Run Club, Nike Training Club, and consumer apps, Nike's researchers and data scientists are busy figuring out how to enable that

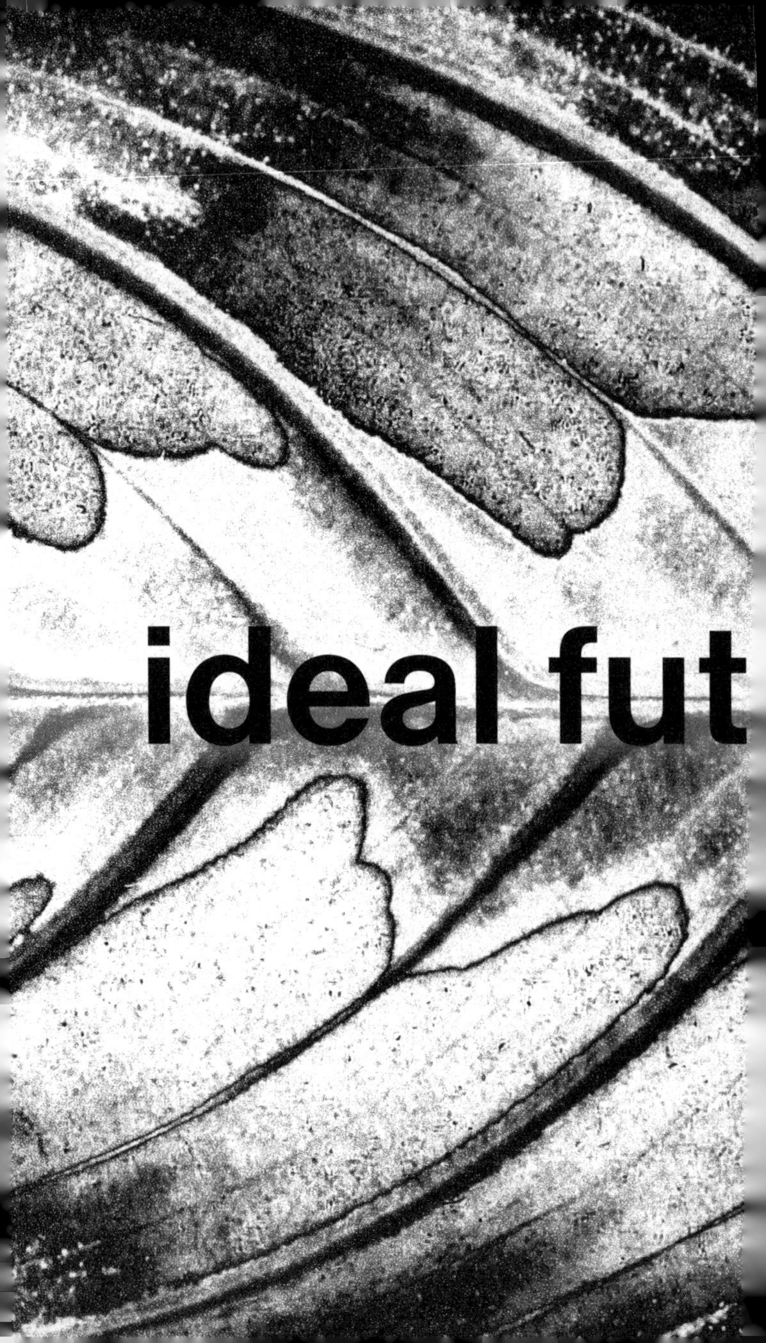
ideal fut

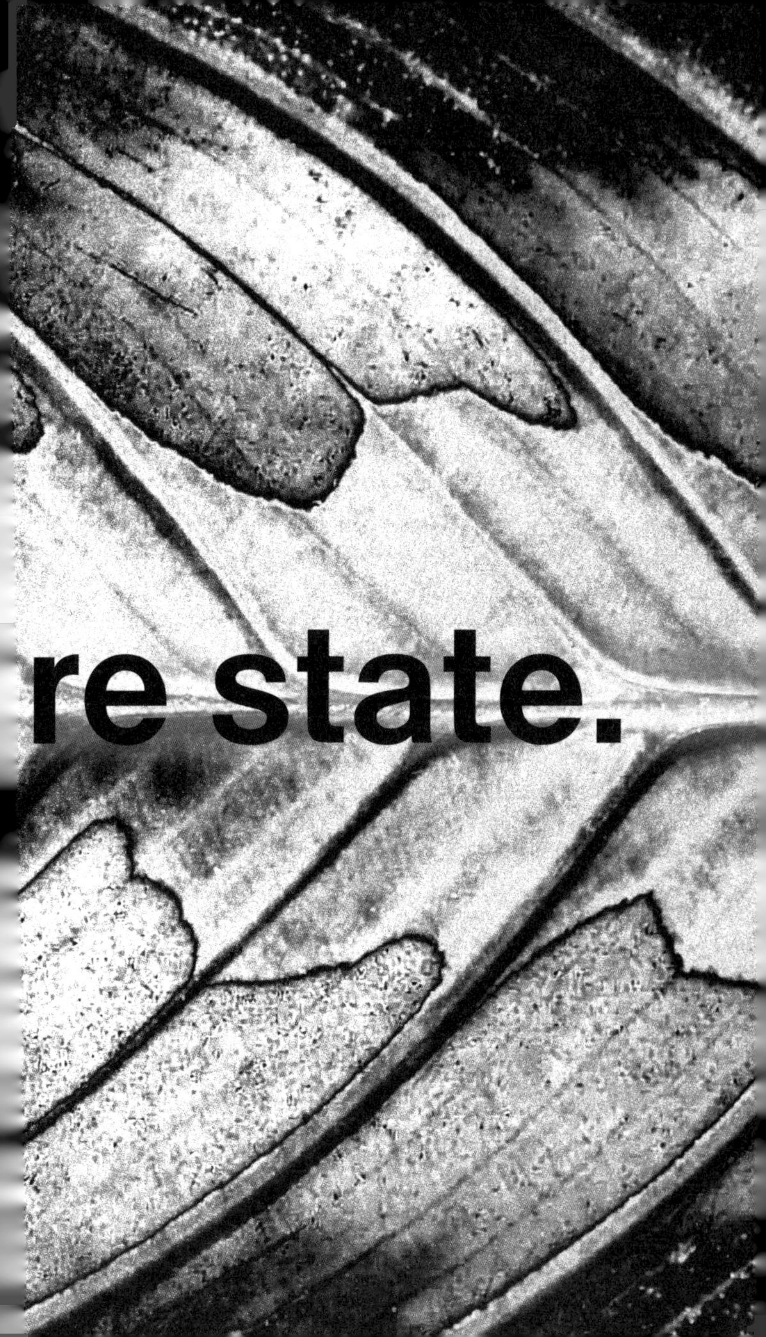
re state.

To do so, they begin by asking, "Is the data relevant to us?" Collecting data without turning it into something useful is a waste of all sorts of resources. They then ask, "Is it relevant to an athlete?" If Nike isn't providing a great experience to help users, then there isn't much point. Finally, they ask, "Is it scalable?" It's one thing to be able to gather data in the lab or a highly controlled environment, but building a richer and more complete data set from users out in the field is the key to long-term efficacy and value.

If a potential data stream passes through all these gates, the company's data scientists categorize it within a relatively simple framework. The most basic form of data is descriptive; it helps inform an insight or a picture of the subject at hand. When descriptive data sets are aggregated, they become comparative. Comparative data allows researchers and users to better understand where something sits within a continuum — to know what good or bad looks like and how that might evolve or change over time. Finally, descriptive and comparative data can be trained into predictive models. Predictive data, a veritable holy grail for data scientists, allows for extrapolating from a handful of knowns to indicate what should happen next.

Guided by this framework, the teams tasked with creating this universe are trying to figure out how Nike harnesses data streams to share a journey with each customer — and how that experience could be of even greater value to the user than to Nike.

As with any question of building new organizational capabilities, one way to view the problem is through the lens of human resources. Shaping this robust ecosystem will entail roles that have never before been part of Nike (or any company, for that matter). Nike's business cards of the future may well include titles like

Perception Explorer, Insight Architect, Sports Neuroscientist, A.I. Linguist, Motivational Psychologist, Sensor Designer, and Nutrient Coach.

But before any of that comes to pass, Nike will need to lay the foundation for understanding what kind of data will meet the criteria above and how to collect and process it. Then, the data must be applied in ways that lets users begin to see and feel the tangible benefits of participating and becoming part of the story.

This is, unquestionably, a design problem. As far back as 1978, the iconic designer Ray Eames said, "We have a tremendous capacity for gathering and storing data; but our skills at modeling data — making it mean something — are way behind." As Eames understood so well, that technical groundwork must ultimately be in service of the end user. It has to add up to a tangible benefit: in this case, supporting happier and healthier human beings. One of the most fundamental truths the NSRL has found is

when people move,

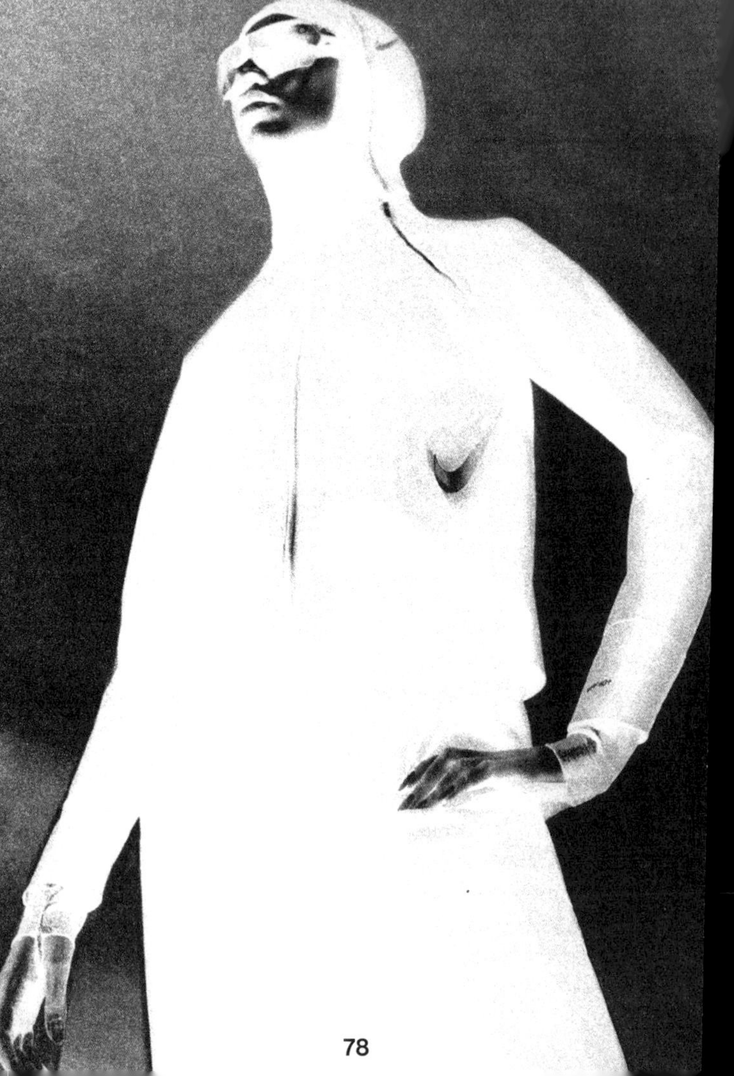

their physical health improves,

and their mental health improves with it.

Over time, one can foresee the line being blurred to the point where customers stop being seen as customers and become so enmeshed in this ecosystem that they're viewed as essential participants and co-creators, with their data serving as a foundational building block for the company's products, services, and experiences. Meaning-making will become a self-reinforcing feedback loop in which customer involvement helps Nike get better at serving customers, and Nike helps those customers get better at doing all the things they want to do.

While that world isn't difficult to visualize, it's a far cry from how we engage with sensors and data today. We have all kinds of ways to stay informed on all kinds of subjects, but relatively little insight into what's actually going on with our bodies on a deep, granular, and measurable level.

Our smartphones may be incredibly sophisticated devices, but from a data scientist's perspective, they offer a relatively crude view of us as points traveling on a map, at a particular elevation, or near another object. Strap on a watch, and now you're adding a greater degree of fidelity by layering in heart rate, calories burned, or BMI — and you can start to create comparative data sets that illustrate your overall health and activity (as the company has attempted to do, going all the way back to the 1987 Nike Monitor).

Now imagine your whole body enmeshed in sensors. The entire NSRL might fit into the sole of your shoe or be woven into your windbreaker or tights. A lens of some sort may track your eye movements and determine your tiredness or stress levels. A reading from the ear canal could infer mood from the sound of your breathing or voice.

Who better than Nike to help you understand your body, with its many interconnected systems and infinite cues and clues, as a map to your fullest potential?

The big unlock down the road may lie in using these sensors, data streams, and feedback loops to harness intrinsic motivation or help induce a flow state during athletic performance, as evidenced by Nike's current content lineup. Some recent headlines include: "Should You Eat Breakfast Before or After a Workout?," "5-Minute Meditation — Movement and Visualization to Fuel a Better Future," and "Harness the Power of Your Menstrual Cycle."

Today these kinds of articles inform readers with tips and suggestions. But squint further ahead, and it's not difficult to believe that, with the right data in play, each of us could be interacting with individually personalized products and services to meet us in that specific moment: a workout that's fine-tuned to our current physiological, metabolic, and hormonal state; a guided meditation or coaching session designed to help us meet short- or long-term goals; a product whose colors change in response to our unique psychic needs.

Another clue toward how Nike might approach building this world lies in the way the company approached its Breaking2 effort to enable a sub-two-hour marathon. The Breaking2 team looked at every aspect of the entire race — including the runners' physical and mental capacities, their shoes and apparel, diet and hydration, the track, time of year and day, pacing strategy, and so on — to find micro-improvements that would cumulatively add up to the desired result.

In the context of "make sport a daily habit," a similar tack could be taken by examining the myriad aspects of movement, whether that's not moving enough, moving in the wrong ways, the best time to move, and so forth. Coaching cues fed with the right sensing data would know when it would be a good time to go for a hard workout versus an easy one, or even offer suggestions to prevent injury or improve technique. There's a whole host of cumulative one-percent changes that could affect how somebody feels throughout the day.

Now pretend all that physical data gets paired up with feedback about a user's mental state or outlook (say, before and after accepting a nudge), and it's even easier to see how Nike could start to build predictive models that tie physical data to psychological results.

In 2020, human beings generated 2.5 quintillion bytes of data per day.

By 2025, it's estimated that 200-plus zettabytes of data will be stored in the cloud.

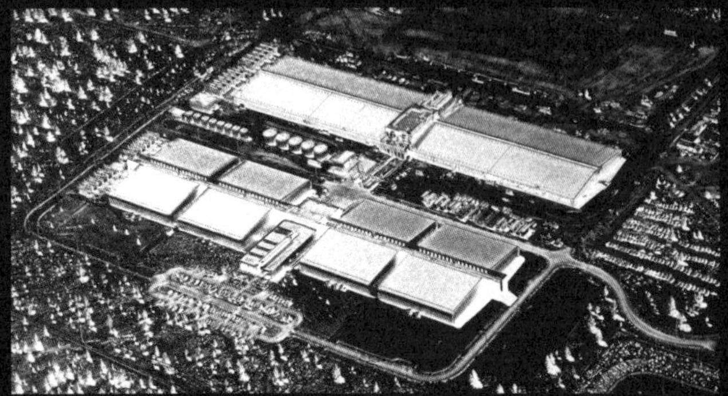

As the physical and digital worlds increasingly merge and the internet or metaverse simply exists all around us, all the time, one can only assume these numbers will keep increasing.

At the same time, the mysteries of the human body are receding. Given the rate at which sensing and data-processing technology is advancing, it's not impossible to believe that we will soon understand the human operating system just as well as the operating systems on our devices.

Nike is already primed to harness these data streams into insights that are actionable for all athletes — to help us help ourselves. Whether you want to walk a mile or run a marathon, the same principles apply. Who couldn't stand to benefit from understanding their mind and body a little bit better? If you already trust Nike to supply you with a shoe that helps you run faster and more safely, chances are you'll trust them to help you better understand your needs, define your version of best,

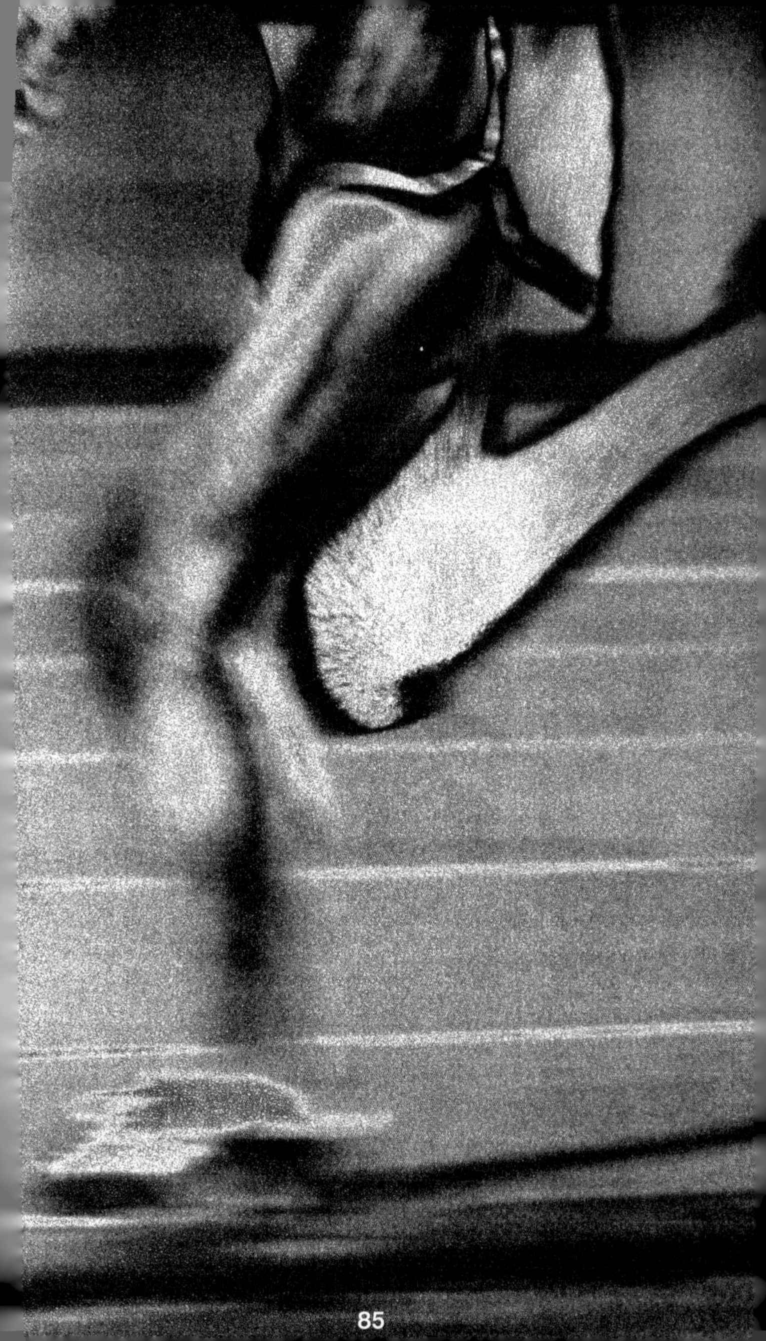

and realize the promise of your full potential.

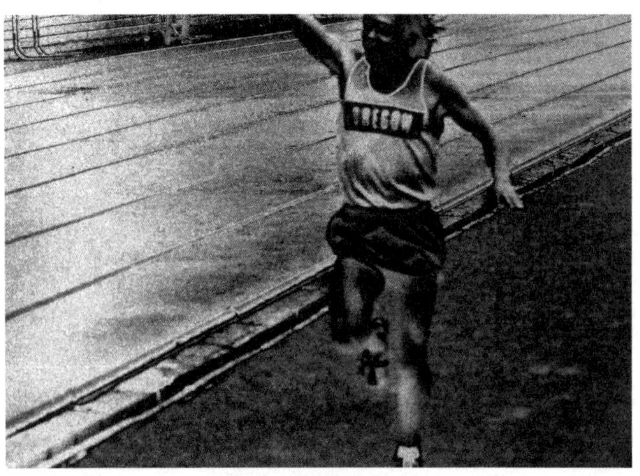

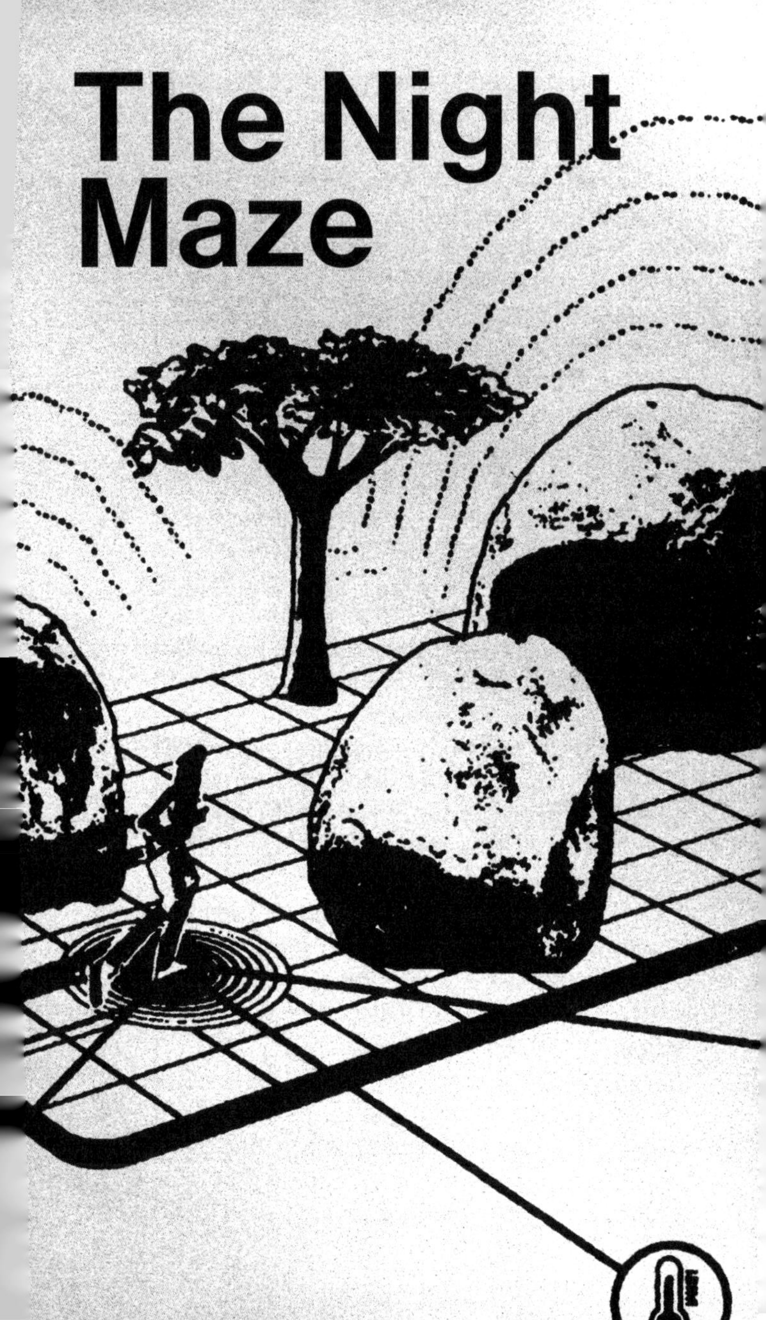
The Night
Maze

"We relax in here," she said to Noah, the rookie power forward and recent college champion, leading him out onto a large viewing platform. It was 25 feet off the ground, surrounded by Oregon forest, constructed from thick planks of hardwood, all painted evergreen. Black squares marked paths to follow and suggested places to stand. Noah went straight toward one and took in the view; an enormous maze spread out on all sides.

He pulled the goggles off. "What is this?"

They were standing next to each other in a Chicago office. Outside was broad daylight.

His host removed her goggles as well and studied him. She didn't answer right away. "Usually our athletes don't linger there. They hear the word 'maze,' and they want to solve it. They think it's just another game. But when you see it — when you go down and really walk the maze, when you take it in, remembering to think and breathe — it does something to you."

She could see Noah wasn't convinced. "The maze is online 24 hours a day," she explained, "but it's open to anybody. Not just our athletes. It's there for stressed-out executives, high school kids, moms with insomnia." She laughed. "And it is definitely most popular at night. People, even elite athletes like you, log in at 1 o'clock, 2 o'clock in the morning. We change the maze paths often enough to keep things fresh, but I'm not even sure that matters anymore."

"What's it for, though?" asked Noah. "Exercise?"

"Of a different sort, I guess. It's just here. That's it. Whether you need time to drift a little, or whether you need space to focus, to meditate, to concentrate. The mind is the most overlooked part of an athlete's training."

Noah already knew all that — most of his preparation was devoted to staying calm and focused — but a *maze*? His skepticism must have been obvious, because she watched him for a moment. "Go try it out," she said. "Seriously. Don't worry. I'll be right here. You won't get lost."

He put the goggles back on.

For the first few minutes, Noah thought he had the place to himself. The maze was silent except for his own simulated footfalls on gravel. The walls around him were too high to see over, adding to the sense of solitude, but he noticed that the paths were growing increasingly large, eliminating any chance of claustrophobia. Soon enough, it didn't feel like a maze at all, but more like a private garden. (He'd later learn that the dimensions of the paths never changed, that it was all a mental thing, a projection, and that was the maze's point: walls and limitations are often only in our heads.)

As he walked toward the bubbling waters of a fountain ahead, Noah realized he had companions. Other people, digital figures, were relaxing in the shadows or quietly walking alone. He even recognized some of them. There were athletes from other sports — football, skiing, offworld games — even a former teammate. He waved. Their digital avatars waved back.

In the darkness, his host's voice startled him. "As you can see, it's easy to lose all track of time in here."

She told him he had been inside for half an hour. He was stunned. The maze had already had its effect.

"It's okay," she assured him. "That's what we want. We want you to use the maze to *relax*. We want you to forget about the world. The maze is not a competition — not with other athletes, not even with yourself. Then, in the end, once you've spent some time inside, going outside again, taking the goggles off, it's the perfect reset."

They spent several minutes sitting on a stone bench together in digital stillness, just enjoying the calm, the virtual light of a setting sun visible through the canopies of pine trees, softly reflecting off the maze's simulated paths.

Later that night, long after he had taken the goggles off, after he had stopped exploring the paths in silence, all Noah could think about was the maze. It had grounded him. It felt therapeutic. He slept better that night than he had in months.

Product to Platform

It began with

the Air Max,

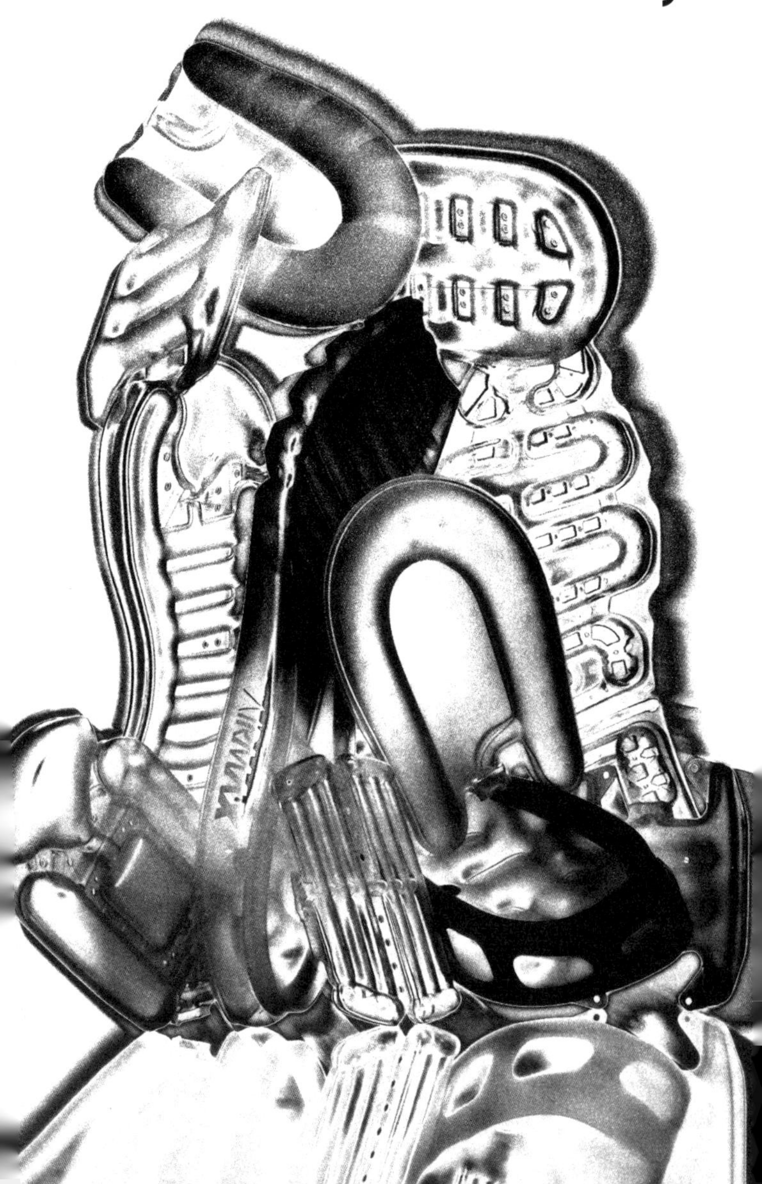

a groundbreaking product that changed the way the company approached design and, in turn, the way the world thought about athletic shoes. It culminated in *Just Do It*, an advertising campaign of such distinction, relevance, simplicity, and power that it has defined the Nike brand ever since. These hallmarks materialized during one of the most pivotal periods in Nike's 50-year history — the year between March 1987 and March 1988 — and it's now nearly impossible to think of Nike as Nike without them.

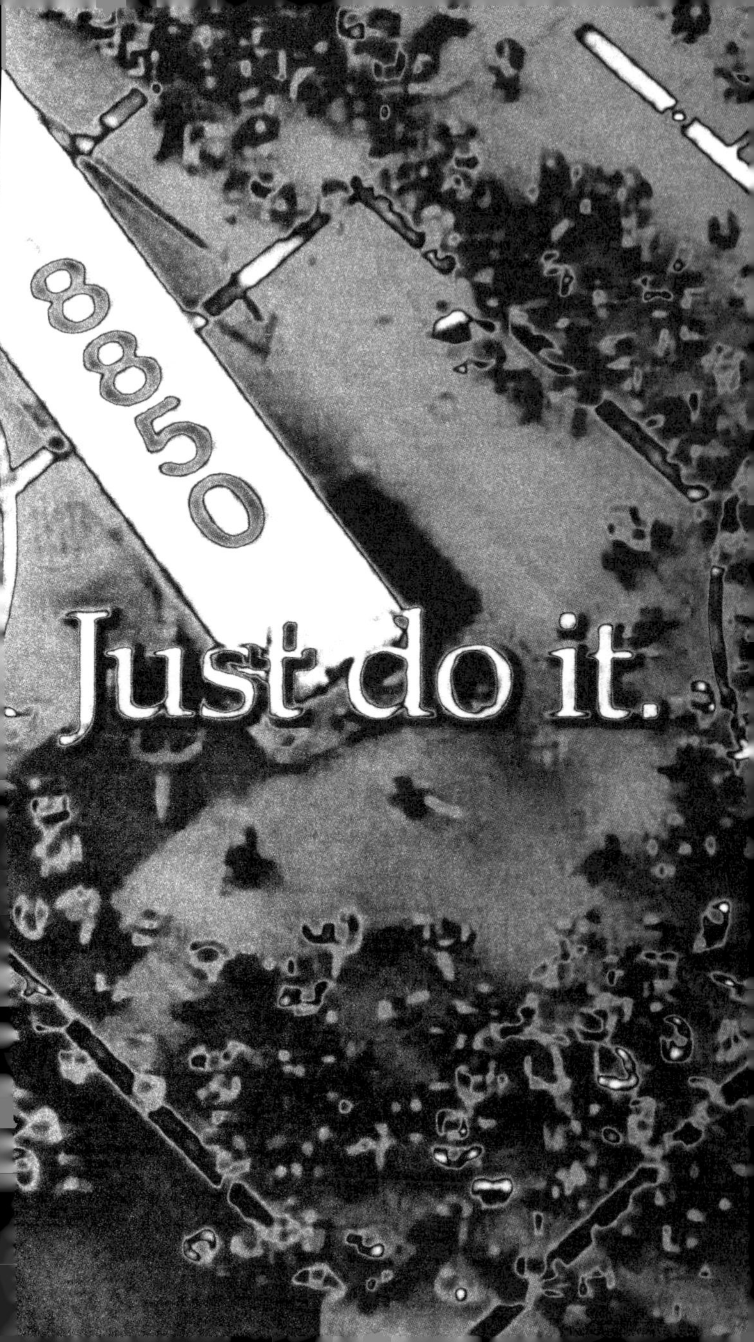

8850

Just do it.

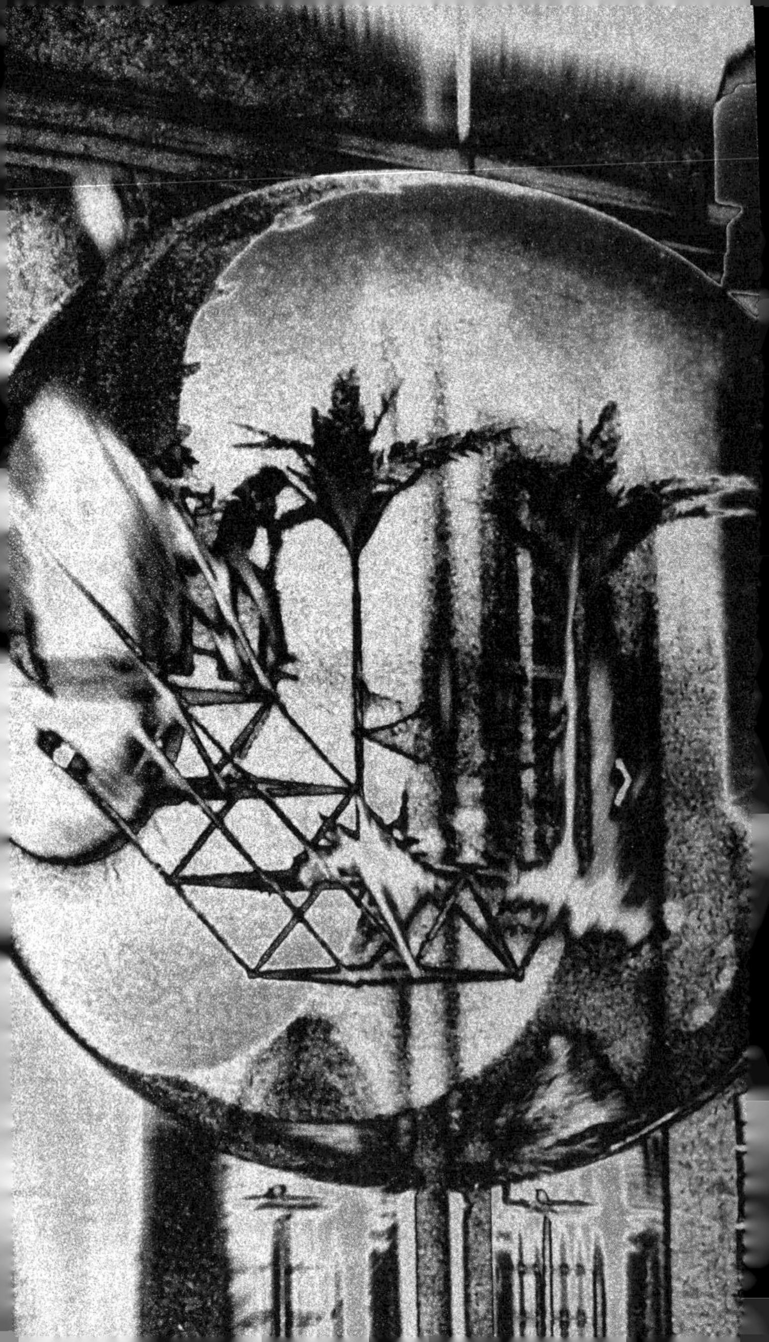

It's equally difficult to believe that these milestones came at a moment when the future of the company was anything but certain. Competition was fierce, sales were down, and a sizable chunk of the workforce had to be laid off. It's possible, however, that it was exactly that adversity that drove Nike's teams to challenge themselves,

upend conventional wisdom, and do things differently.

Air Max was a different kind of product. Sure, it was a top-of-the-line performance running shoe that harnessed the Bowerman DNA, but it was also a design with a story to tell. Air, Nike's proprietary cushioning technology and flagship innovation, had been utilized in certain footwear models since 1979, but unless you read the fine print, you probably wouldn't have known or even cared. With the Air Max, you could feel it and see (through) it. The product instantly communicated what it was all about, and when you wore it, it said something about you too.

With *Just Do It*, the formula Air Max set in motion with a singular product got layered onto the entire company. Nike wasn't just about selling you stuff; the stuff was a gateway to your own inspiration and aspirations, athletic or otherwise. No matter your skill level, interest, or ability, *Just Do It* harnessed a universal message of self-improvement and self-actualization, speaking directly to the voice deep in our heads.

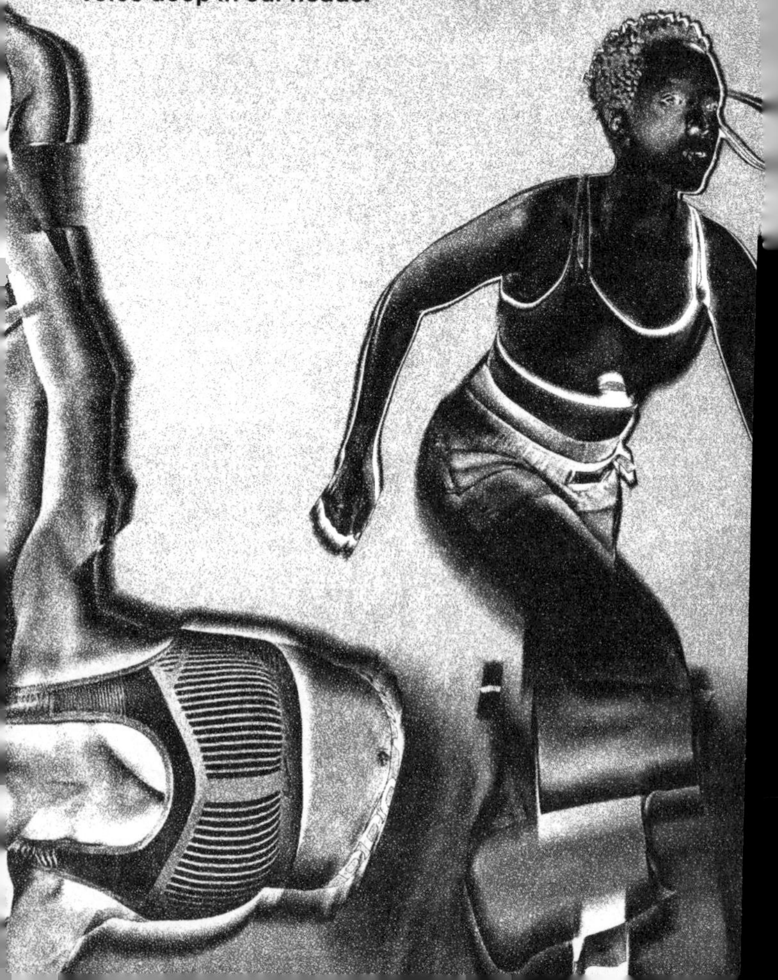

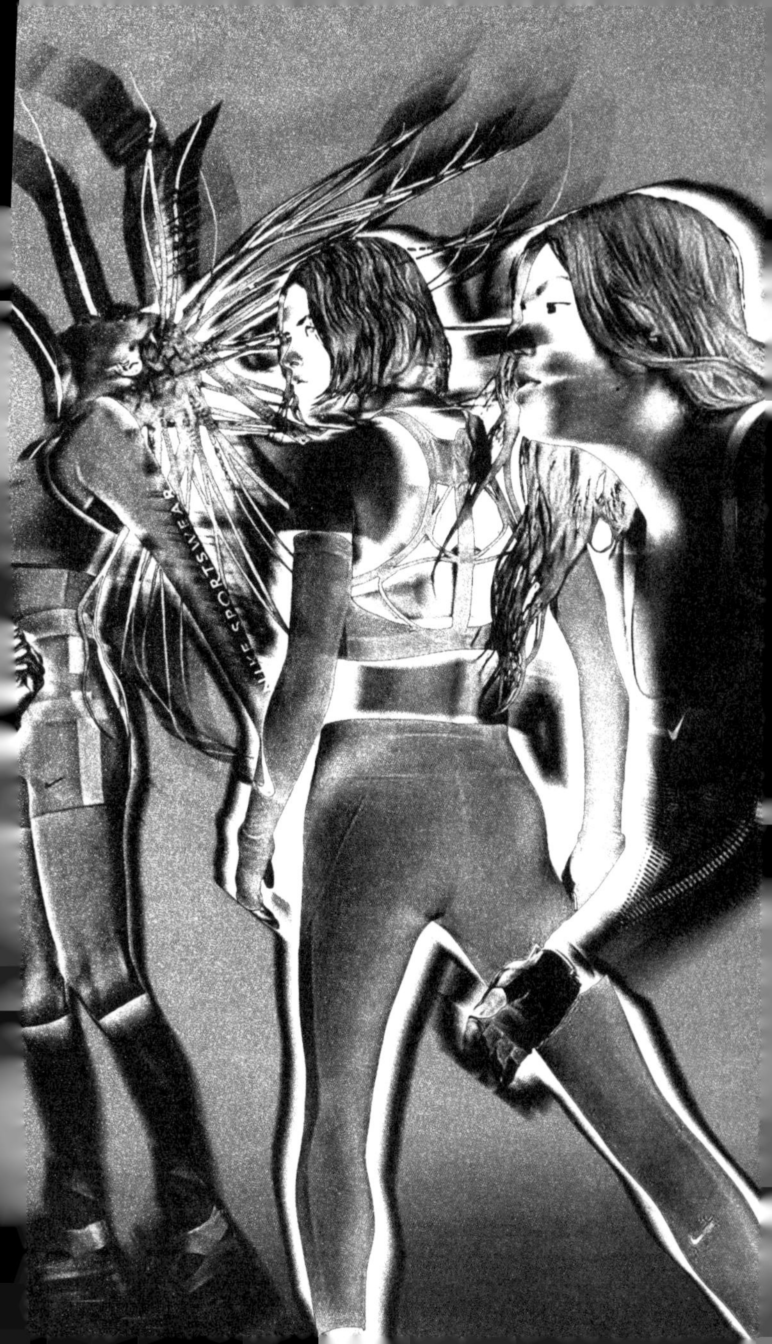
SPORTSWEAR

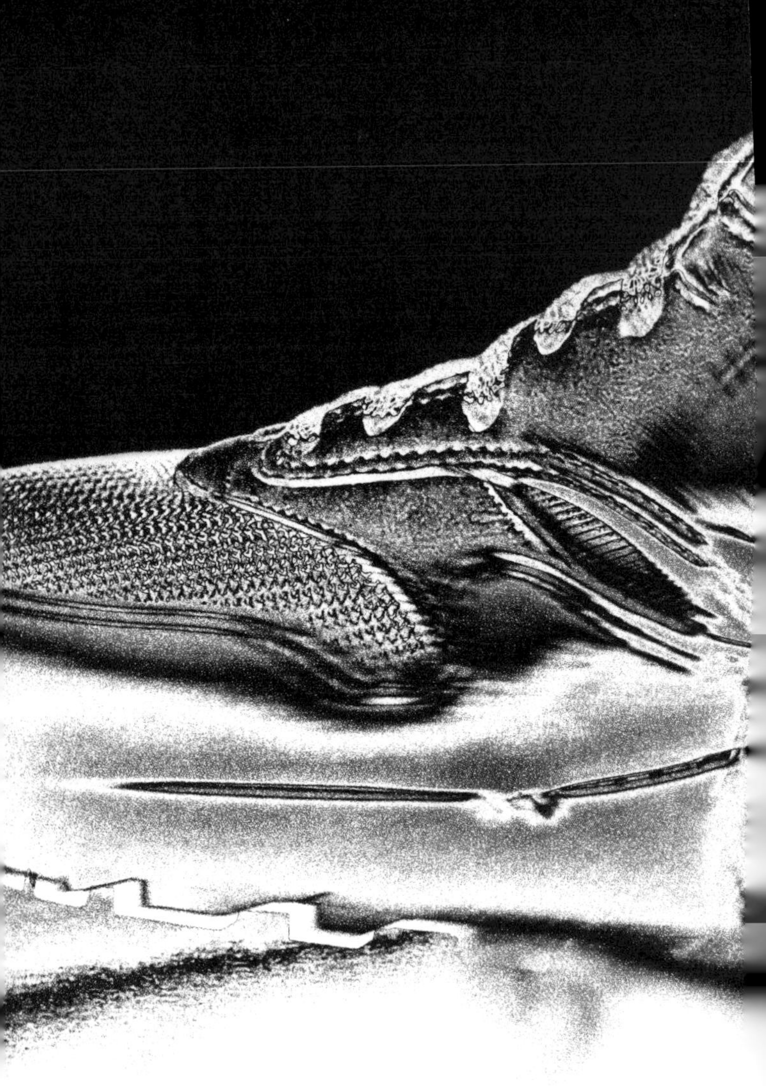

The fact that the tagline quickly became synonymous with the brand attests to its effectiveness not only in communicating what Nike is all about, but also in enabling just about anyone to see themselves in Nike.

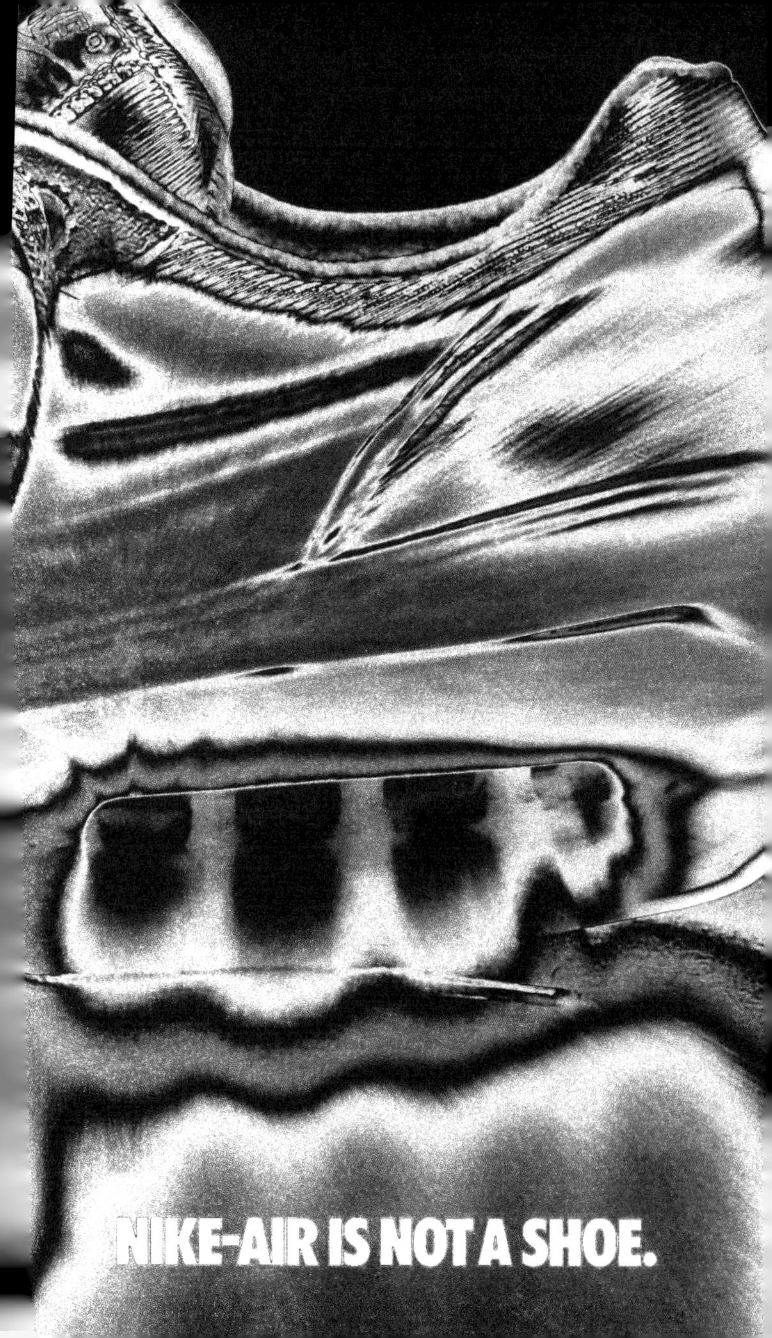
NIKE-AIR IS NOT A SHOE.

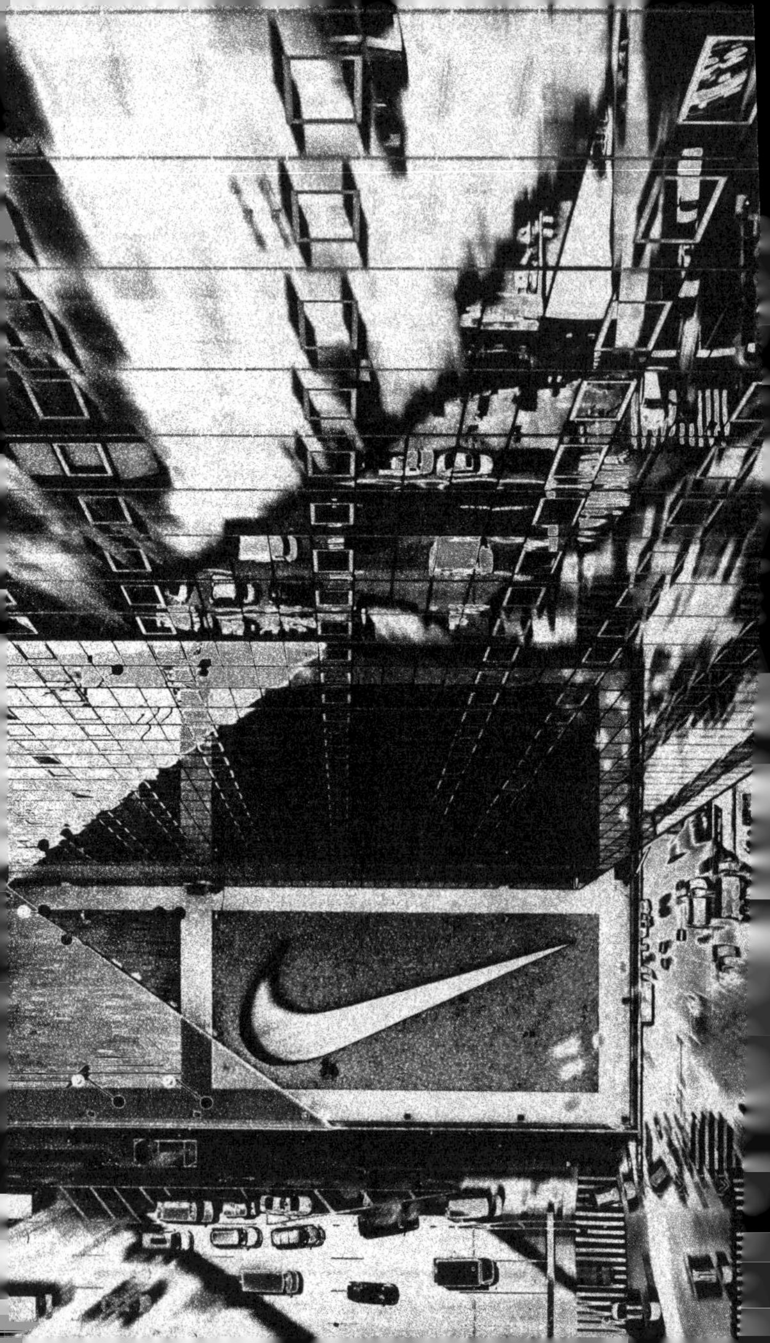

Almost immediately, the signature technological innovation of Air Max — visible air — got adopted and implemented across multiple categories and product lines. In the ensuing decades, Air has undergone countless reworkings and reinventions that are driving new typologies and continually improving levels of performance (alongside significant reductions in environmental impact). The Air Max served as the template for Nike's approach to product design — in which science-based, technical performance standards are seamlessly wed to an impactful visual story — and has gone on to become an ever-expanding concept that has continually adapted and evolved as Nike has grown. The same can be said for *Just Do It*, which remains as fresh as ever.

Appreciating the role of Air Max and *Just Do It* in shaping the Nike we know today is critical to understanding where the company goes from here. These pivotal benchmarks serve as consequential precedents for how Nike operates internally to harness innovation and feed the design process as well as how it engages externally with its audience and brings more and more people into the fold. With even a cursory overview, it becomes clear that both have transcended their origin points of product and campaign to become platforms.

A platform is open-ended and multidimensional.

A platform, as a kind of interface, implies and relies upon the experience of interaction.

A platform can be based in technology and offer means of accessing, distributing, and improving upon itself as that technology advances.

A platform is relational and serves as a multidirectional conduit to information, tools, ideas, creativity, and each other.

A platform offers a foundation for growth and change.

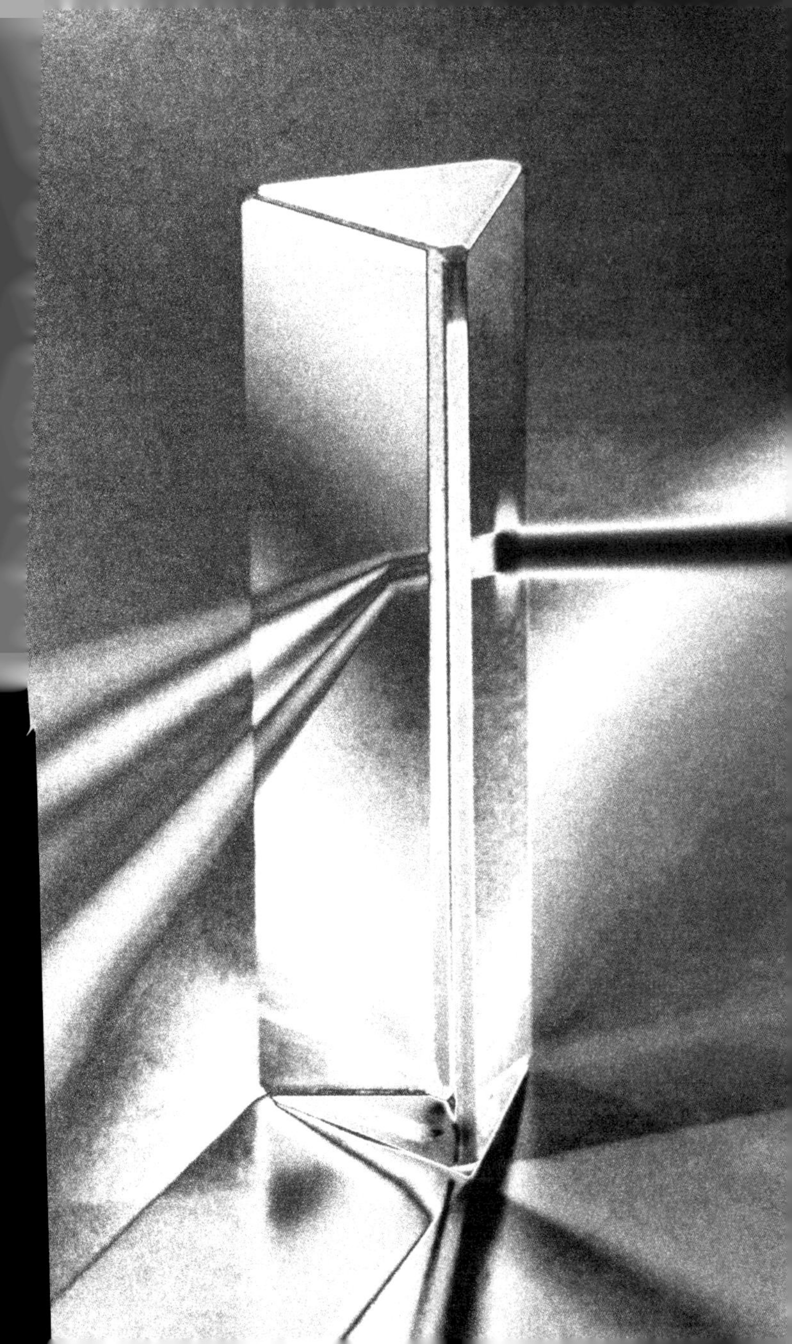

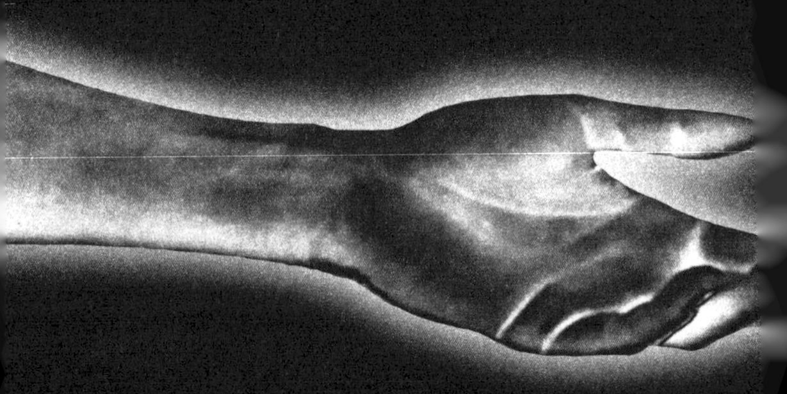

In the days before Air Max and *Just Do It*, platforms were gated and inaccessible. Relatively few people decided what we watched on television or listened to over the airwaves. Access to information — through print media and resources like the yellow pages or research portals in libraries and institutions — was limited. But today, in almost every arena of life, technologically enabled platforms have become interwoven with the fabric of our existence. We can connect seamlessly to anyone, anywhere, and anything at any time and in any place.

Within this new landscape, Nike is itself evolving from a provider of goods and services to a platform for delivering innovation and inspiration to every athlete in the world. Within the company, platforms are increasingly integral to new ways of working and creating, and they enable new forms of relationships, knowledge-sharing, creativity, and collaboration to emerge from the experiences they offer. These internal mechanisms drive new outcomes within the organization, offer new possibilities for external engagement and relationship-building, and inform the feedback loop of progress.

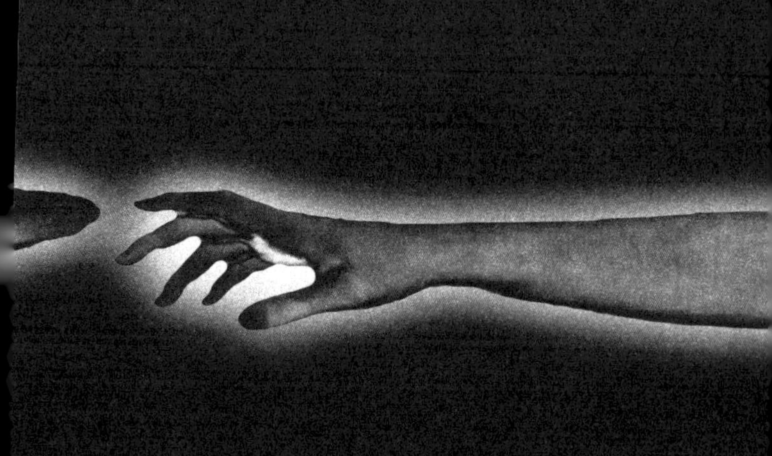

**connect to
anyone
anywhere
anything
any time
any place**

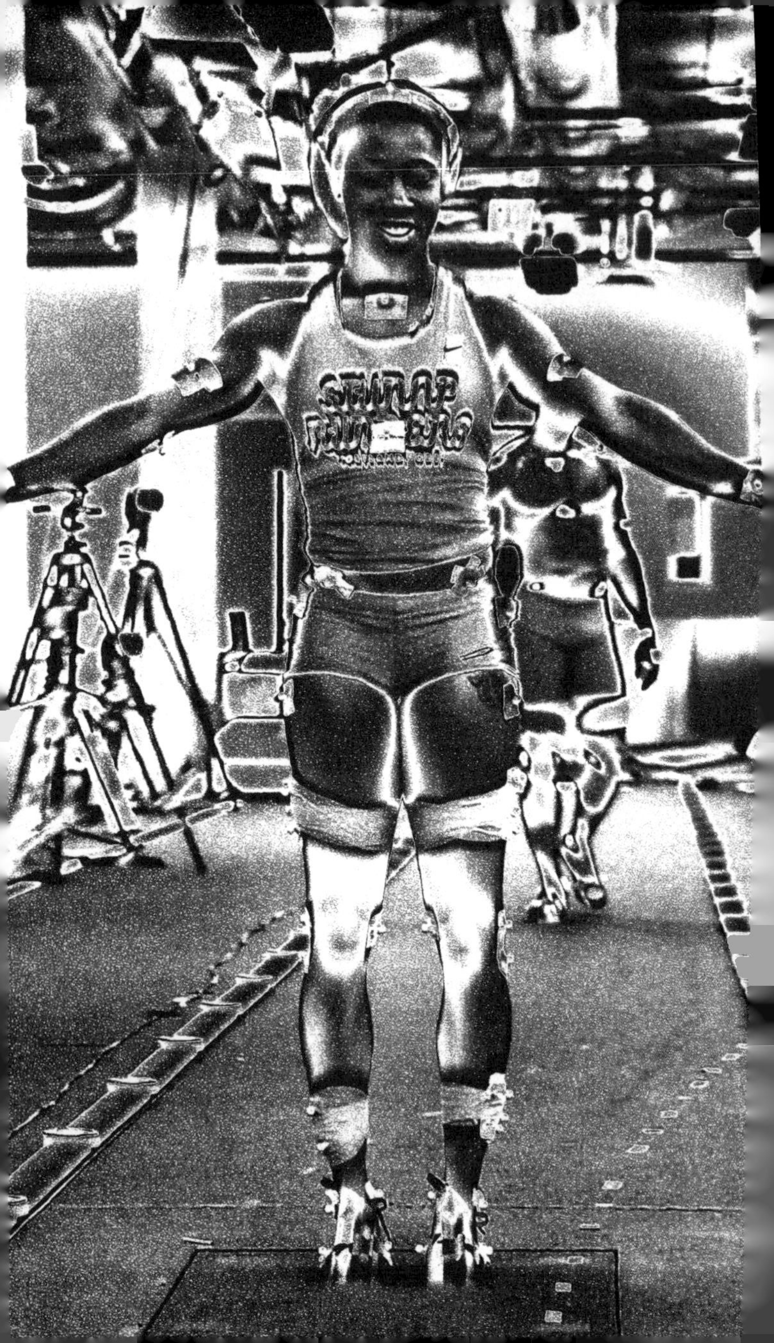

Since the days of Bill Bowerman, the key driver of design at Nike has always been data. Collecting both quantitative data (*How much weight could be taken out?*) and qualitative data (*Did it feel good to wear?*) and applying any insights derived from that information to the next round of design has been the basic premise behind the company's product for decades.

That process — which was at one time modeled by a 1:1 relationship between, say, a University of Oregon athlete testing out a track spike and Coach Bowerman hacking away at it in his workshop — has since developed into a prodigious effort fueled by one of the world's largest and most sophisticated sport research facilities and the contributions of thousands of athletes, designers, engineers, and problem-solvers of all stripes.

Despite Nike's astronomic growth, the role of the designer remained largely unchanged in this cycle. It was their job to serve as the interpreter of the data, deriving insights and applying them to an industrial design via decisions grounded in performance characteristics, materiality, and aesthetics, then guiding that design into existence through a web of supply chains and manufacturers in such a way that would satisfy the needs of the market and enable the next round in the cycle. And then, in 2016, a single product amidst the thousands Nike made that year pointed to a new way forward.

The shoe in question was a size-5 Zoom Superfly Elite created for defending gold medalist Shelly-Ann Fraser-Pryce to be worn in her 100-meter race in the Rio Olympic Games. The new way forward involved a different kind of participant in the design process: an algorithm.

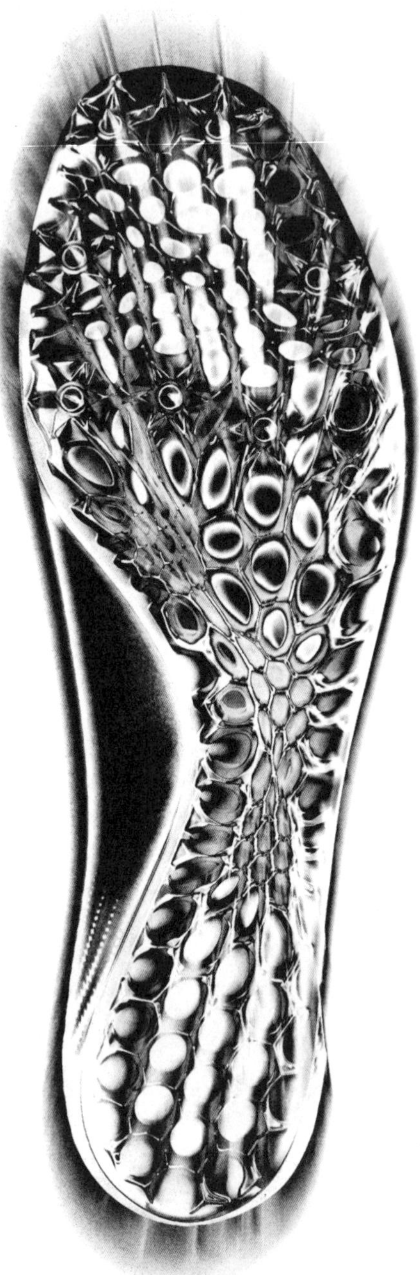

Borrowing techniques and tools from the forefront of the architecture world, designers at Nike fed data culled from five-time world champion Shelly-Ann Fraser-Pryce's foot strikes and shape into the computer to determine where the shoe's plate should offer flexibility versus stability, balance coverage with weight elimination, and guide the placement of the spikes for maximum traction.

By initiating a set of rules for the computer to follow rather than working toward a singular, fixed outcome, the designers soon had hundreds of variations to evaluate and manipulate. Moving seamlessly from digital files to rapid prototypes, they were able to test and evolve their designs in a matter of days instead of the customary weeks required for overseas samples.

In the ensuing years, Nike has built upon this first foray into computational design to the point where the capabilities reach across all kinds of footwear and apparel and into almost every product category. While athlete data from the NSRL was always the lifeblood of Nike design, it now connects more seamlessly and tangibly to product through the design and fabrication tools the team has put in place. It's also fundamentally reshaping the role of the designer in the process.

Whereas in the past a designer might start with a sketch and work with developers and suppliers to bring a physical form to life, the computational design process offers near-endless variations and starting points. By harnessing the potential of algorithmic design, parametric modeling, and machine learning, designers at Nike are essentially

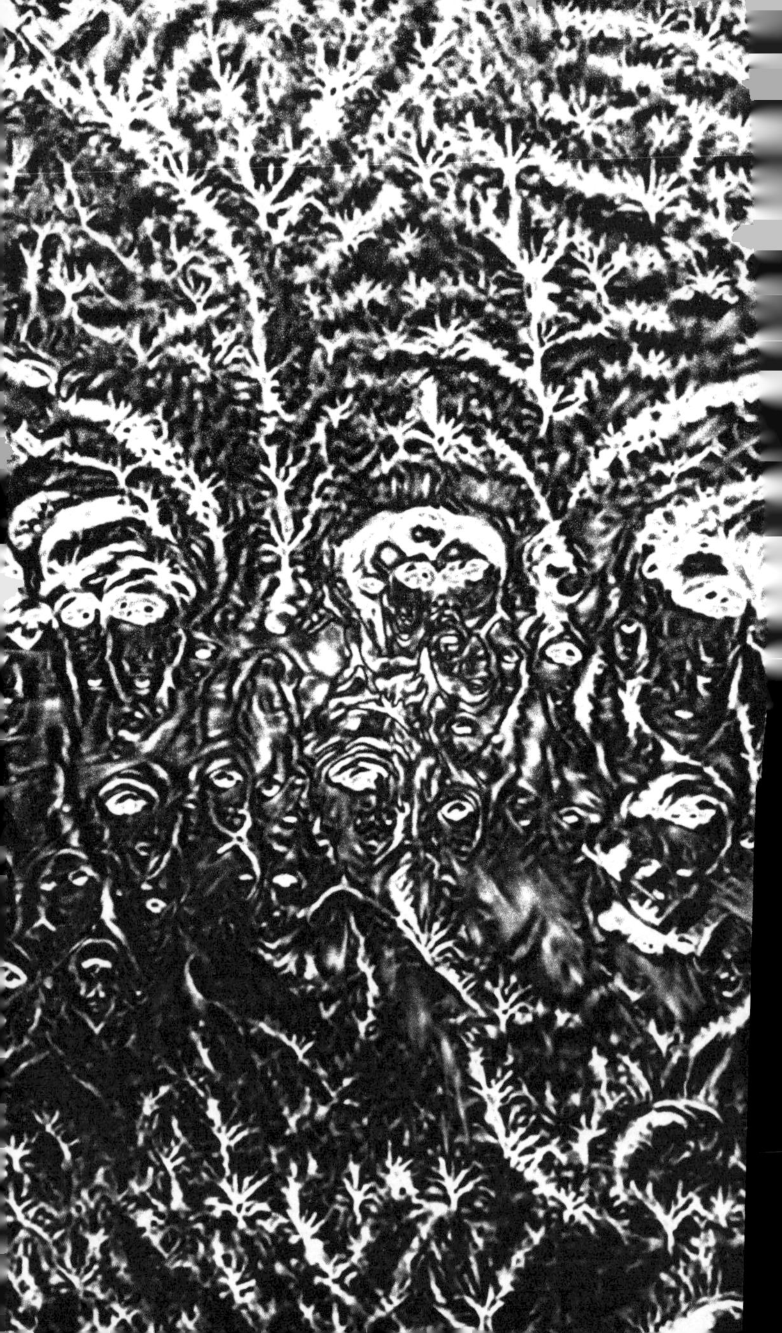

asking the computer to dream.

Informed by a widening physiological and kinesiological data set that accounts for human and environmental factors like sweat and heat maps or surface and weather conditions, the computer and the designer can work together to co-create something that's beyond the limits of human imagination and manual design tools.

By filtering and manipulating the data that's fed into the model and mapped onto the product, the designer operates more like the conductor of an orchestra, finding nuance and identity in the dialing up or down of certain elements as they guide the algorithm toward a solution (or set of solutions) that embodies their desired characteristics.

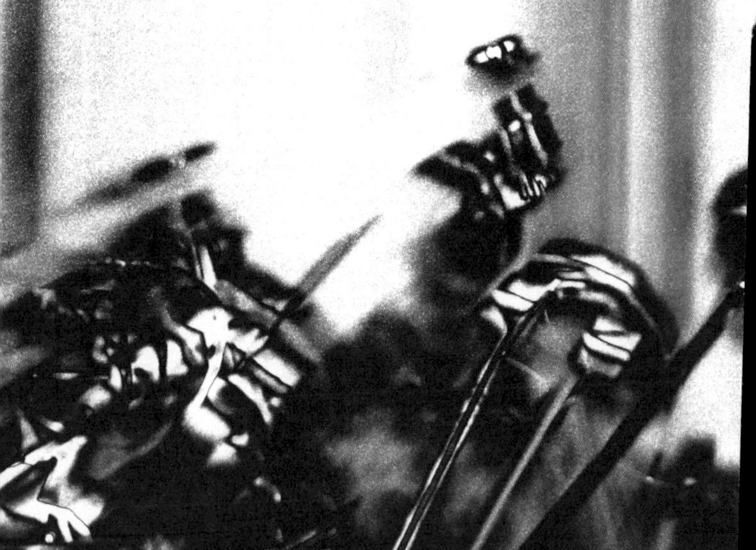

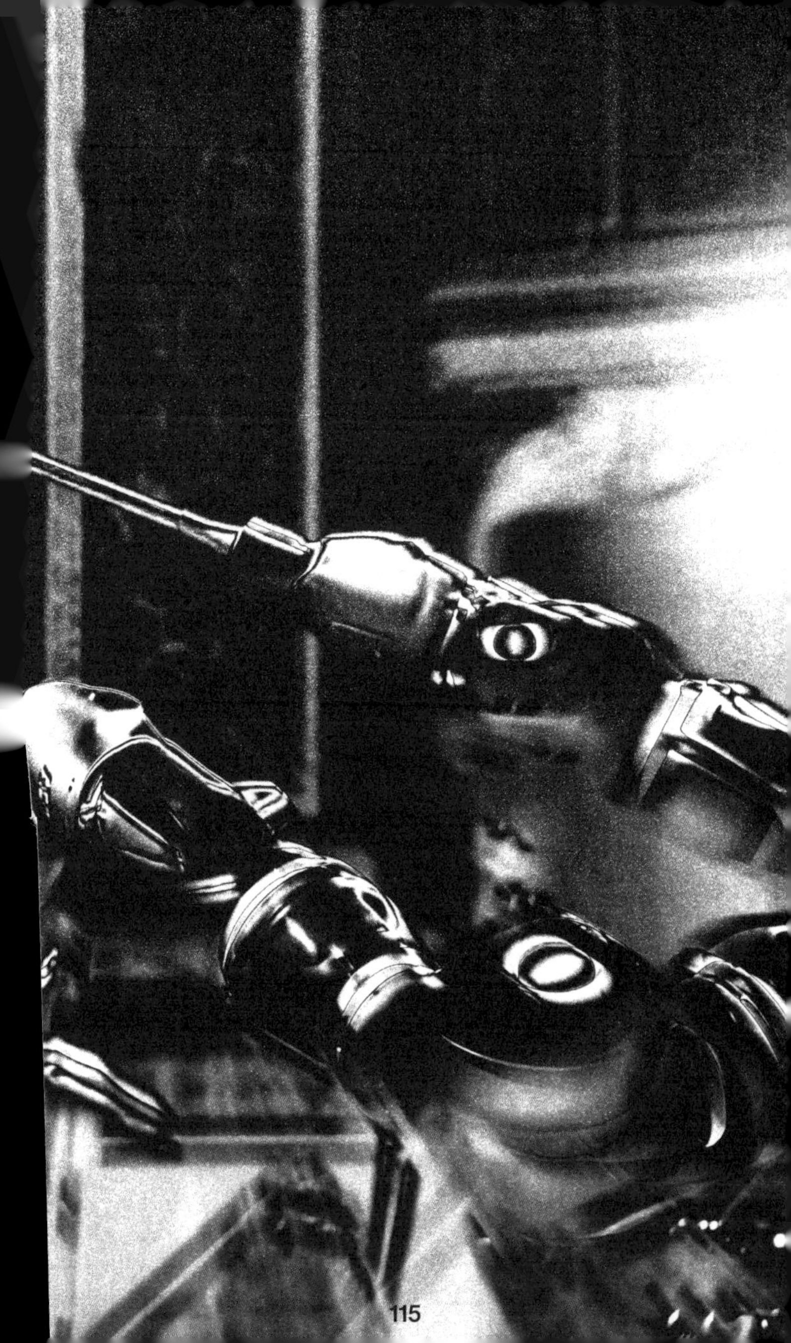

Though some people might hold the perception that these digital tools would serve to displace the designer, reality has proved otherwise. In the process of growing this capability, Nike has added more people to the design process and involved more disciplines as the models have grown to encompass a wider variety of needs.

From an R&D perspective, these tools are a worthwhile investment that helps create differentiated product and separation in the market by more impactfully incorporating insights into finished designs. From an artistic point of view, the ability to harness completely new patterns, textures, and forms offers endless inspiration and has led to bold aesthetic leaps. From the broader organizational view, the current toolset is just the beginning of something that's shaping up to be far, far greater.

While the current computational design team is something like a specialized unit that gets called in to lend their abilities to specific projects — a traction pattern for basketball footwear here, a new chassis for global football jerseys there — the future Nike envisions will see these tools become the universal platform for all design.

The advantage to this is that you not only reap the benefits of harnessing science and data to inform better performance outcomes, you also begin to create a connected library, or ecosystem, of design assets that everyone can access. As this system takes shape, it will represent one of the most significant transformations in Nike's history.

With every design, hundreds of decisions get made that lead to the finished product. Every decision results in the creation of knowledge that informs the project at hand, the next project a designer might work on, or an adjacent project in a completely different realm. With the creation of a new digital platform for design, the knowledge-sharing that used to be passed between employees by word of mouth or happenstance (and just as often was lost) would instead be facilitated within the design experience itself. Those decisions, and the outcomes of those decisions, would all be captured and available for any Nike designer to work with and learn from.

This also implies that the design process can begin further downstream and require less ground-up effort with each new endeavor. For Nike, that means the foundational elements of designing a shoe, shirt, or pair of tights remain consistent and inform an improving base layer of standardization. What it doesn't do is force the designer to adhere to any particular creative output. Building off a standardized foundation only augments the potential available to individual designers, meaning more time can be devoted to pure exploration in pursuit of innovation.

Another important feature of a digital design platform is that it connects Nike designers to the science and data upstream, to each other's creativity and ideas, and to the product-creation process itself. As Nike develops the tools to bring this vision to life, the physical testing and sampling process is becoming increasingly virtual.

Already, software is able to analyze how materials come together and predict how they will perform under certain conditions or in contact with human bodies in motion. These predictive modeling capabilities will surely develop to offer even richer fidelity and the potential for even greater experimentation. And when the product is ready to be made, the platform will communicate seamlessly with the machines that will produce the physical item. After all, a design for industry is also just a set of instructions.

At any point in the design process, if something sits outside the realm of possibility in the supply chain, the system could immediately correct for it to ensure viability. As the world transitions away from subtractive design to more automated, additive, and demand-driven manufacturing models, the system can be tuned to use materials more efficiently or facilitate access to innovative techniques and capabilities as they come online.

Today, Nike designers talk about being able to work at the "pixel" or "voxel" level. In the future, they could be working at the molecular level, manipulating or even creating molecules that currently don't exist into wholly

new vocabularies of materials and objects.

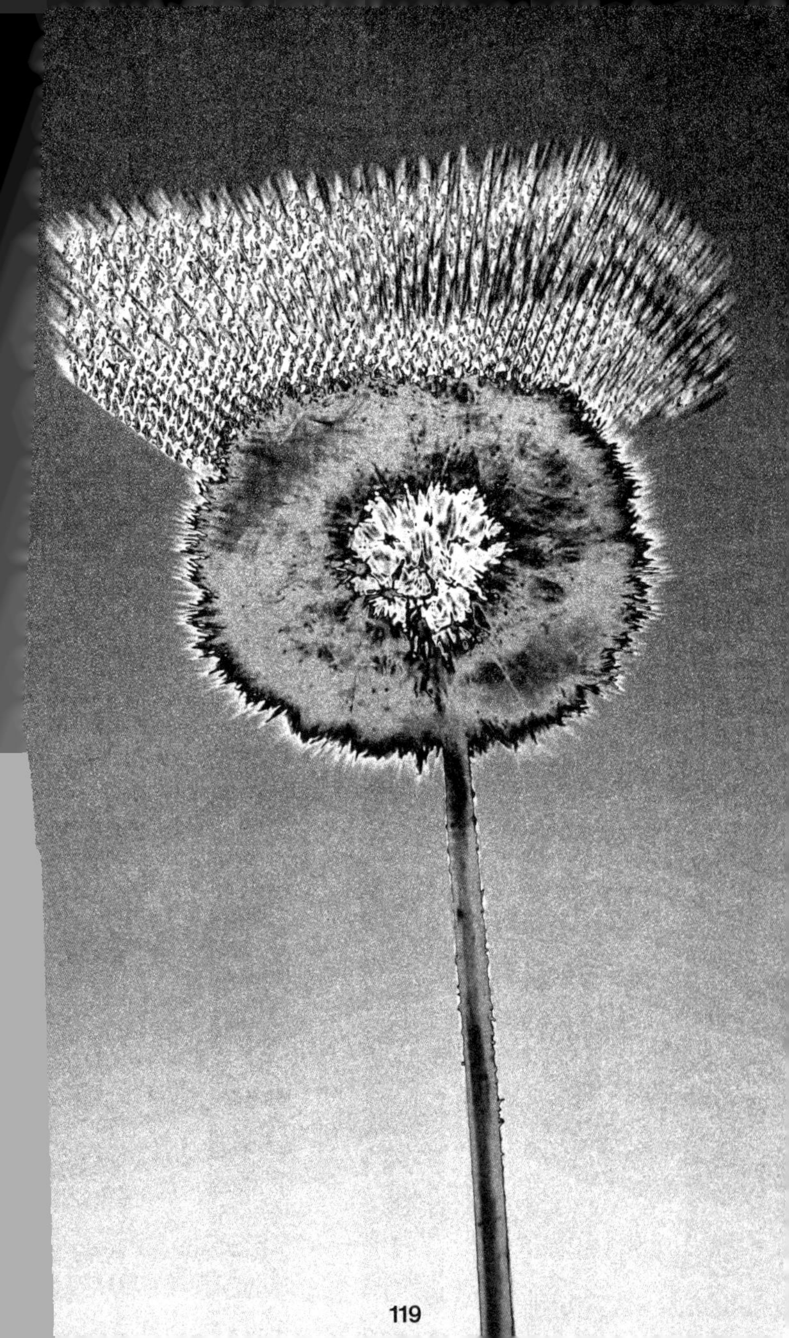

The effect of implementing these systems is to shift toward a significantly more conscious and intelligent approach to design that offers new avenues for creation, exponentially enhances the ability for iteration, and — by closing the gap between those who make the product and those who use it — facilitates a deeper understanding of the product's impact. That might, for example, be the psychological impact,

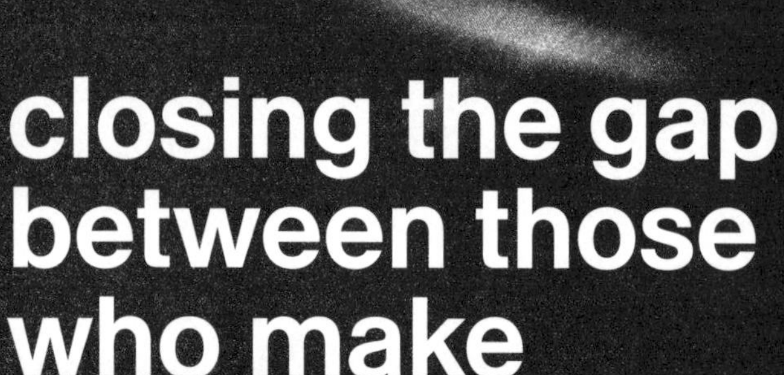

closing the gap between those who make

environmental impact, or market impact, all of which become factors the designer can directly and meaningfully engage with earlier in the process. In this way, the profile of the future designer is extremely different because they are integrating these elements and synthesizing them into designs that first meet the parameters of society at large, then the parameters of individuals.

and those who use

Essentially, Nike's design platform also becomes the ultimate bellwether for consumer tastes and trends as well as a forum for collaboration and community-building on a scale beyond anything we understand today. A platform built to link knowledge and ideas within the company can just as well be used to make connections to people outside the organization, opening the door to a greater diversity of designers and design approaches. Beyond design, as Nike grows into a 21st-century brand with a presence in both the physical and virtual worlds, the organization itself will ultimately become more of a platform as it enables new expressions, experiences, and forms of collaboration. The company is already smoothing the way for this effort.

The idea of who those collaborators will be and how athletes could participate in informing, inspiring, or co-creating with the company will continue to change as these platforms evolve.

In one direction, that means connecting to a system where it's easier to make things locally at a smaller scale more attuned to local needs. In another, it means reassessing what happens inside and outside of Nike to consider giving people an opportunity to participate more deeply in a network of new ideas and knowledge.

In another, it could be creating new models for generating equity and moving from co-creation to co-ownership.

Whatever direction the future takes, it's clear the relationship between brands and their customers will transform as technology enables new forms of interaction and interpolation. The transactional relationship of the past — you buy our product, we take your money — isn't enough. Younger audiences expect more from the brands they engage with. They want them to show up and be part of their community: to offer shared values, to build together, to be part of the story.

And the reality is, with access to the right tools and technology, people are going to do all these things with or without brands. They're going to create their own communities, their own content and creative expression, and even their own markets. So instead of directing their business *at* the customer, the question becomes how a brand like Nike can exist *around* customers in ways that are inspiring, productive, and purposeful.

In this new world, building platforms that interlink the entirety of Nike — spanning pure research and data science, material exploration, product creation, customer engagement, and community-building — is key to extending the values that the brand has spent the last 50 years defining, evolving, and refining.

If successful, platforms will put all that innovation and ingenuity in the hands of every Nike designer and every athlete in the world.

The promise of *Just Do It* won't just be a promise; it will be a few clicks, swipes, taps, nods, or blinks away.

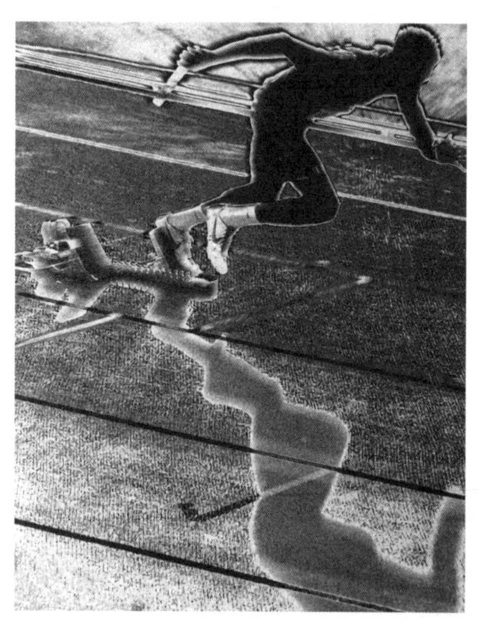

All Conditions Here

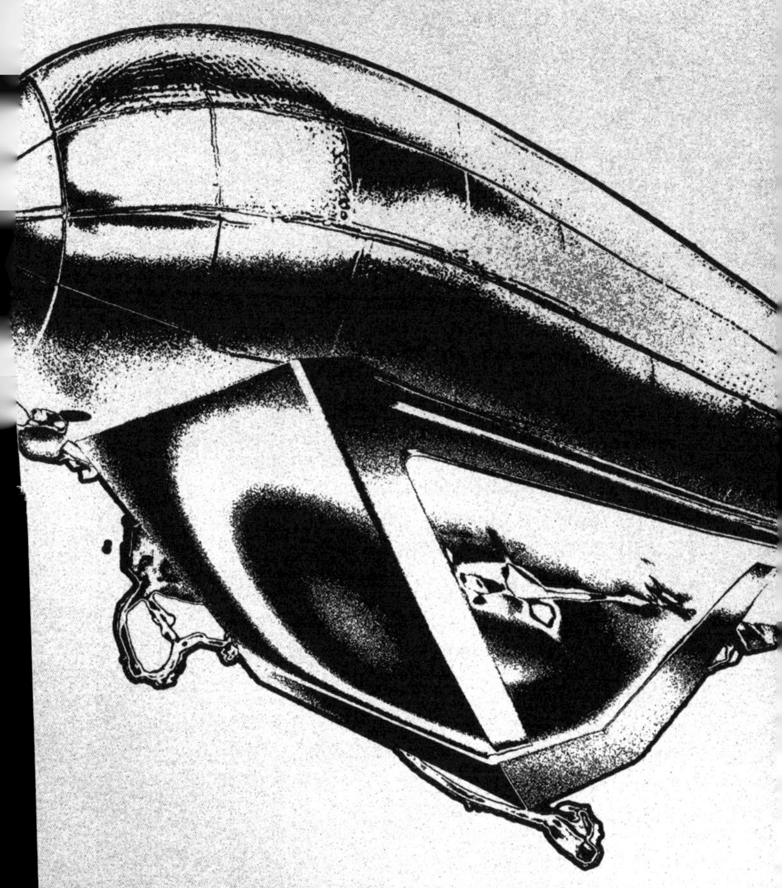

Taking the airship was Jo's idea. She knew an aerial view would give them all a better perspective on their running route, which followed an ambitious new course a few hours outside of Nairobi. Her hosts agreed, and soon enough the group was aloft in a silver dirigible heading toward the race with more than 50 runners on board.

"I'll be the first to say it: you were right," confessed Jo's host, Aria. "This view is spectacular." Coming from the woman who had designed the course they'd be running that day, it was quite a compliment.

While she was no longer competing, in her own day Aria had been the closest thing to a trail-running superstar, known around the world for her courage, charisma, and athletic prowess. She had won ultramarathons in the remotest valleys of the Himalayas, on trails winding across Canadian archipelagoes, even on the streets of Mumbai. But deserts were her favorite terrain. Since her retirement, Aria, with a background in electrical engineering, had become a cross-country course designer, pushing the limits of the sport by wiring new sensing technologies directly into the landscape.

The airship quickly reached its cruising height. Within minutes, they were hovering over the Nike All-Conditions Lab. Dozens of running trails and nearly infinite climbing routes surrounded an experimental ceramics facility in the grasslands below. Inside, computerized clay-mixing labs were developing abrasion-proof coatings for clothes and footwear, as well as huge ceramic plates used to create the route's challenging boulder fields. Each boulder, some of them 30 feet tall, had been carefully designed and fabricated. The ceramic plates helped to capture dew and rainwater, keeping plants and animals hydrated, but they were also kitted out with impact sensors embedded in the ceramics themselves.

"Our clothing and gear now interact directly with the landscape," explained Aria. "The landscape is constantly sensing us." Running there was as much about athletic achievement as it was about medical self-awareness. Nearly every square foot of the terrain was wired to measure an athlete's impact, speed, and direction, as well as body temperature, heartbeat, hydration, and more. Dramatic changes indicating potential injury or heatstroke could be detected instantaneously. "The course gives each runner feedback. It's a relationship, a back-and-forth. Look," said Aria, interrupting herself to point at some human figures far below. "You can see the first group."

The evening's first crew of runners began filing down through a canyon pass. The rocks ahead of them had begun to glow subtly in the twilight. Aria was proud of this: the partially translucent, artificial rocks she had designed for Nike could be illuminated from within, creating a subtle glow meant to keep the trail visible as well as suggest divergent routes for different runners. In the event of a medical emergency, the rocks could also act as beacons, emitting signals of distress for search-and-rescue parties.

The effect was eerily beautiful and had become a signature aspect of the running and climbing routes Aria had designed around the world. (In fact, they looked so good in photographs, her trails had become popular wedding destinations, with glowing geometric boulders spread out around each ceremony like jewels.)

As the dirigible came back to Earth, landing beside the ceramics lab, Jo asked how the rocks were powered. "By the sun," said Aria, "but also by the athletes. Every time someone launches off a rock or lands back on the ground, the course translates that kinetic energy into electrical impulses. The more athletes, the more charged the course becomes, the more accurate the information they can get back from the sensors."

Everyone stepped off the airship onto a flattened grass lawn. The blimp's pearlescent, silver skin reflected the golden burn of sunset, revealing patterns of circuitry etched inside the material. The runners began to stretch, limbering up, focusing on the route ahead. It was a short run, just 30 miles, but they all knew they'd be running alongside its designer. Everyone wanted to impress.

"You know, it's a shame you're not competing anymore," said Jo. "I'd love to beat you on one of your own courses."

"I'm not competing *officially*," answered Aria.

With that, their run began, feet padding across rocks and soil, up a grassy hill, and into their first vast boulder field, its shapes beginning to glow and pulse with their quickening heartbeats.

Sustainable
to Symbiotic

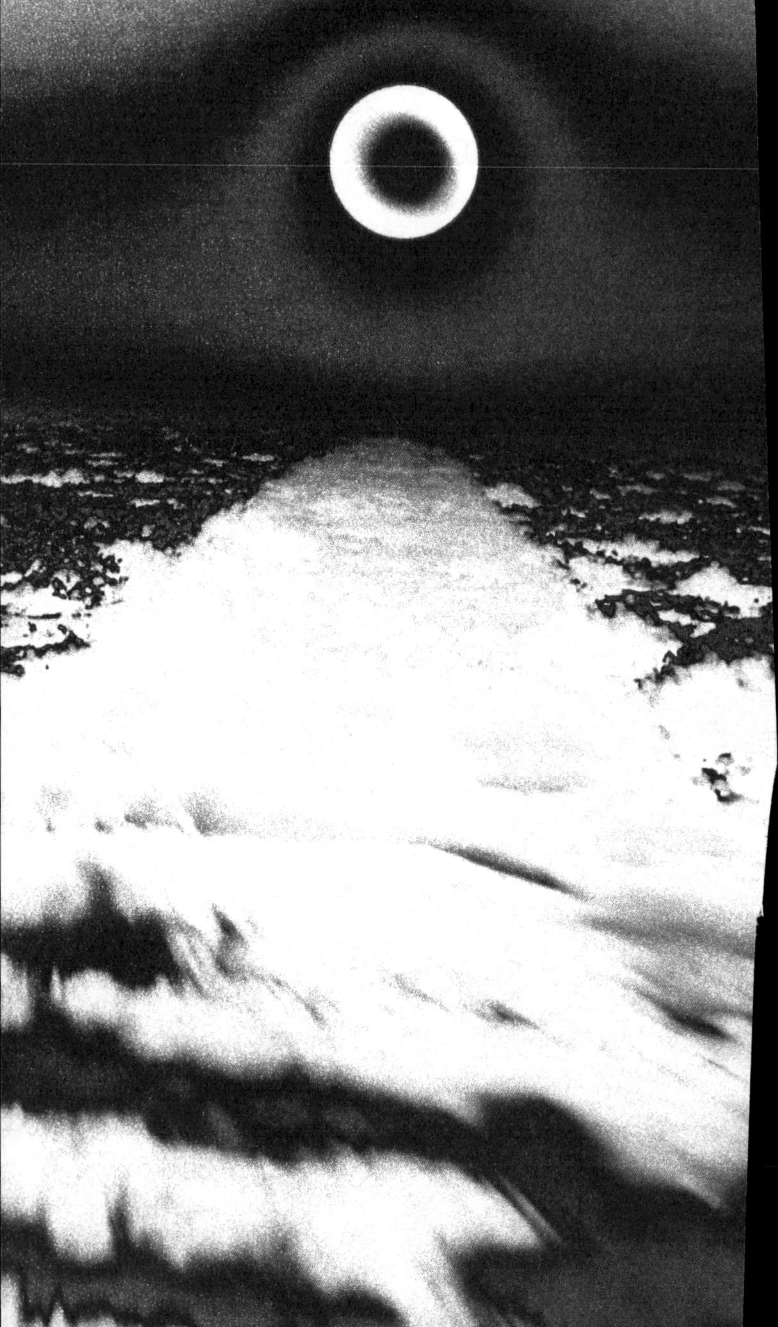

For generations, businesses — and the designers who create the products they manufacture and distribute — thrived on the premise of infinite resources, continual global expansion, inexpensive labor, and maximizing profits. Although our average standard of living and life expectancy have gone up, we've built system upon system, inclusive of energy grids and global supply, that will eventually break when faced with the inherent boundaries of what our planet can provide.

The Earth atop which all this has been built offers its own series of interlocking puzzles developed over billions of years. For all our sentience and accomplishment, humans have been, quite literally, only scratching the planet's surface. Only now are we beginning to truly understand the effects of our environmental abuse and decode the complexity of nature's underlying structures and paradoxes. This is also out of necessity. Increasingly, the Earth is sending signals that we're nearing the limits of our current direction.

For over three decades, in the face of this emerging reality, Nike set goals to eliminate waste, reduce energy and water use, and remove materials that are known or suspected to be harmful to human health. But as great as these efforts have been, Nike knows it needs to do more. By sharing an ambitious vision of net-zero emissions by 2050 and a 30-percent drawdown of its greenhouse gas emissions by 2030, it signaled that absolutely everything it does is open for reinvention. Why? Because

without a
play on
no future

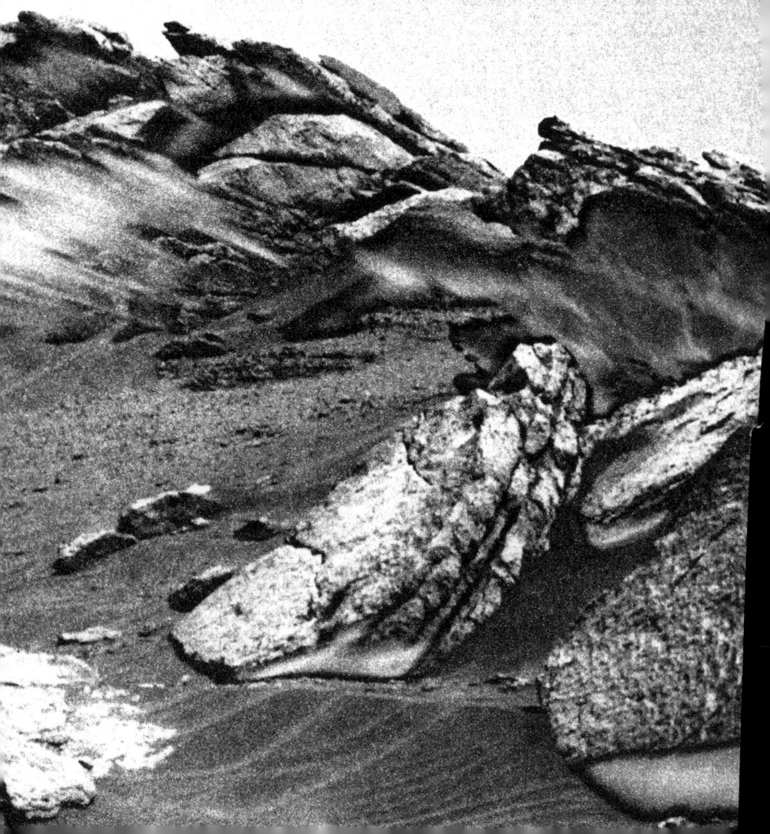

planet to there's for sport.

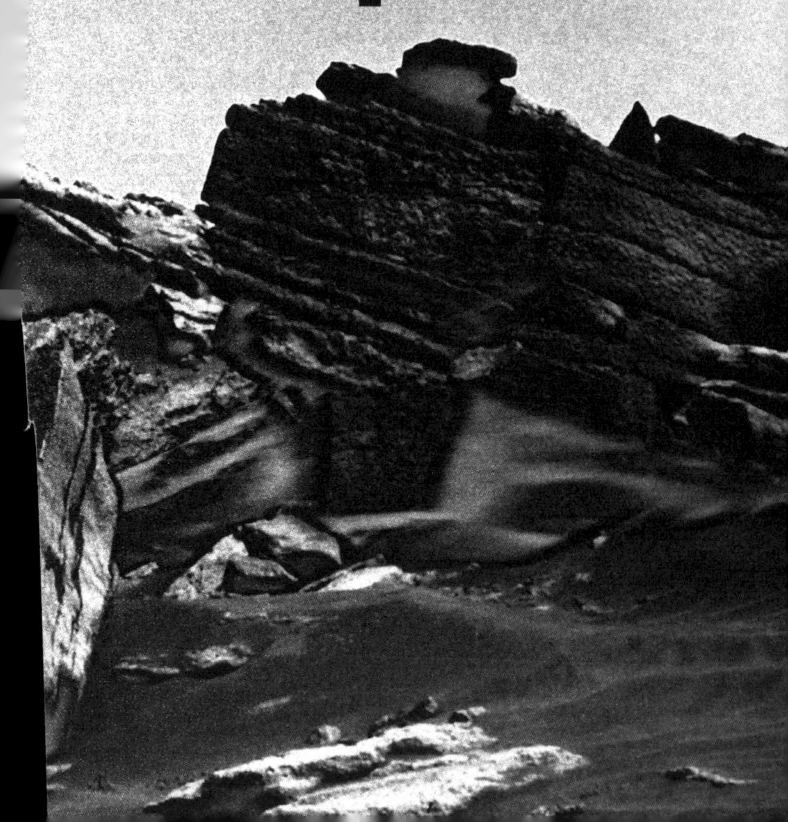

Nike sees a clear mandate there and isn't waiting for legislation, regulations, or customer expectations to draft an agenda.

There is no single answer or approach that's going to solve all the problems at hand. These complex issues demand holistic strategies and overlapping initiatives across multiple arenas and disciplines. What started with a couple of employees on a small team in their own department has become integral to every aspect of the business.

Because the effort is so vast, Nike had to establish clear baselines and benchmarks the entire company could work from, set science-based targets for environmental impact, and develop a strategic framework that encompasses the complete lifespan and life cycle of products.

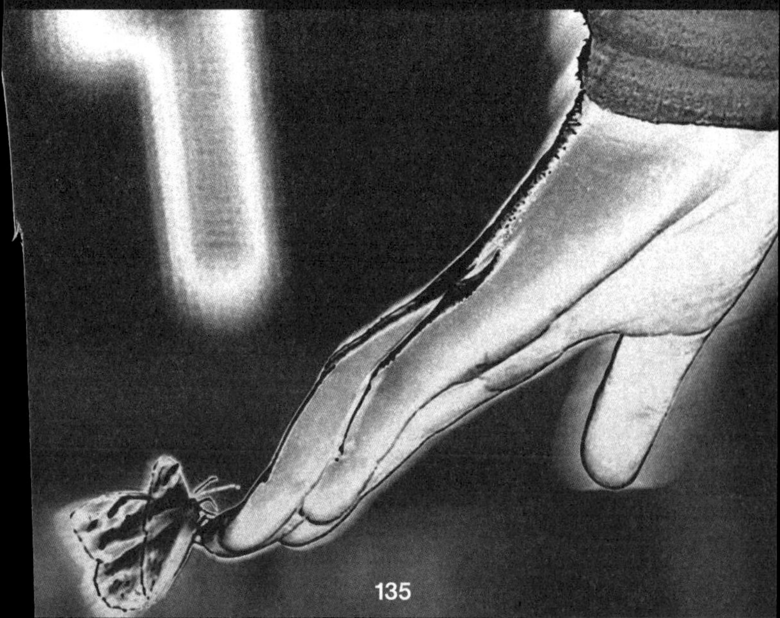

As these approaches were deployed, it proved helpful to categorize three zones of activity: industrial, consumer, and post-consumer. The industrial zone encompasses the design, manufacturing, and distribution of product. The consumer zone is where products reach customers and do what they have been designed to do. The post-consumer zone corresponds to the stages after that product has lived out its useful life. For Nike, each zone plays an important role — individually and in relation to one another — in reshaping the company's entire value chain into a continuous, regenerative system where nothing is wasted. Each zone is also, naturally, rife with opportunities for design.

As important as strategies, goals, and frameworks are, where the rubber meets the road (literally and figuratively) is with materials. As a company that makes stuff, Nike must not only contend with how that stuff gets made, but also realize its ambition of complete circularity, or what happens to that stuff after it's purchased and used.

Materials represent the biggest part of the company's environmental footprint, so they also comprise the area where improvements and innovations can have the biggest impact. Materials play a foundational role in each of the zones outlined above. They are the raw ingredients (or "feedstock") going into the industrial zone. Design is, in a way, the creation of recipes for selecting and combining those ingredients during the manufacturing process.

In the consumer zone, materials are partly what attract us to choose one object over another, and their qualities contribute to our experience of objects as we use them. To make things that people want to put on their bodies and perform to the standards demanded by the world's top athletes requires

materials that are both beautiful and useful.

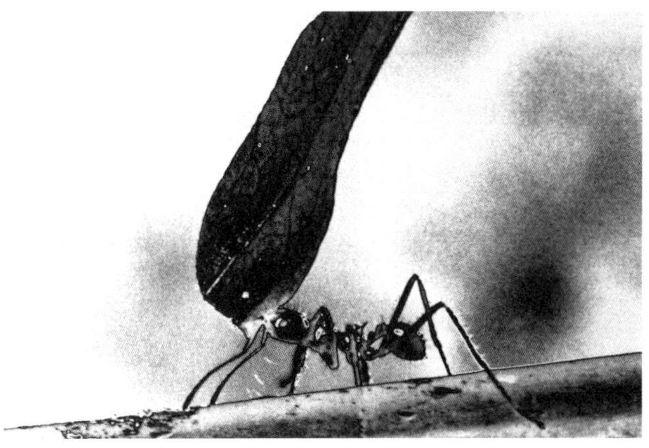

Finally, in the post-consumer zone, the ways those materials can be decoupled, sorted, re-harvested, ingested, digested, and turned back into usable ingredients (either within Nike or elsewhere) becomes critical to closing the loop and eliminating waste.

Nike started its sustainability journey as part of a notoriously wasteful fashion industry, where up to 50 percent of raw materials that go into manufacturing end up as trash before those products even hit the shelf. With traditional rolled goods, no matter how well-optimized the pattern designs may be, cutting and sewing (as with the uppers of shoes) leaves leftover material on the table. Much of the trim from molded foams and rubbers also ends up on the current scrap heap, though Nike aims to change that by 2025.

an exact amount of material

This picture once again points to a multifaceted effort where the materials and the methods by which those materials get formed into product both need reevaluating. For Nike, the future of manufacturing will increasingly rely on additive techniques like knitting or 3D printing where an exact amount of material can be placed in the exact place it's needed. With these kinds of technologies driving product creation, manufacturing no longer has to be something that happens "over there." Rather, with less reliance on traditional labor, smaller, nimbler, more automated operations could be located in every major market or, at some point, even in your own home. All this just relies on getting the right molecules in the right place at the right time.

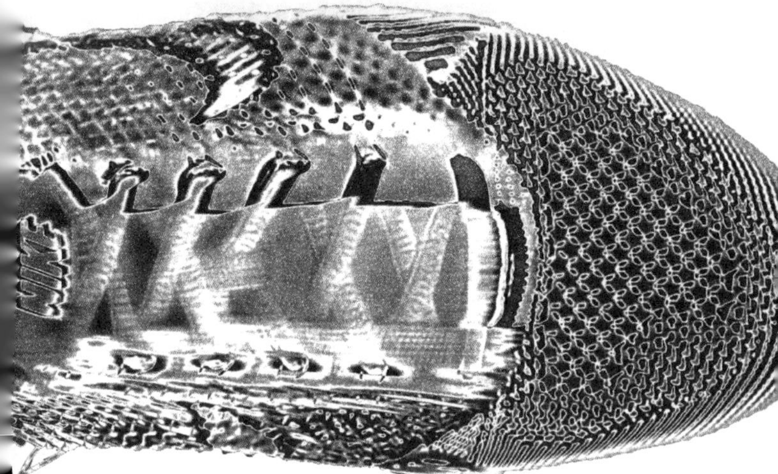

in the exact place it's needed

Everything in our human-made world is basically carbon atoms that have energy added to them to build a chemical scaffolding. We can't make carbon atoms, so we have to go and find them somewhere and then process them into higher-functioning molecules that perform the way designers expect them to.

For decades, these processes and resulting materials have been the domain of the petrochemical industry — think plastics, soaps, solvents, fertilizers, pesticides, paints, rubbers, epoxies, and resins. Global supply chains were built on, by, and for the oil industry without great concern for side effects and contingencies. The unfortunate changes we're seeing to our world are undoubtedly a direct outcome of this willful blindness.

Efforts are underway to reduce the carbon score of every pair of shoes and every garment that Nike makes. To do so necessitates upending the prevailing paradigm of fossil fuel-based, single-use, virgin materials. But if Nike isn't going to extract those carbon atoms out of the Earth, where will they find them?

The first answer is through recycling, which the company has been doing in one form or another for almost 30 years. Since the 1990s, Nike has been producing a composite material, Grind, out of the soles of old sneakers and putting that new material back into its own product or in other products like flooring.

Designers are pushing the boundaries of how much recycled content can be incorporated without compromising any performance properties. Recent endeavors like Space Hippie, a line of shoes promoted with the tagline "this is trash," have taken the recycling ethos even further by incorporating both pre- and post-consumer industrial waste into almost every element of the design. As evidence of how Nike scales innovation, Space Hippie's radical recycled design vocabulary has been deployed across entire ranges of product, from classics like Air Force 1 to entirely new models.

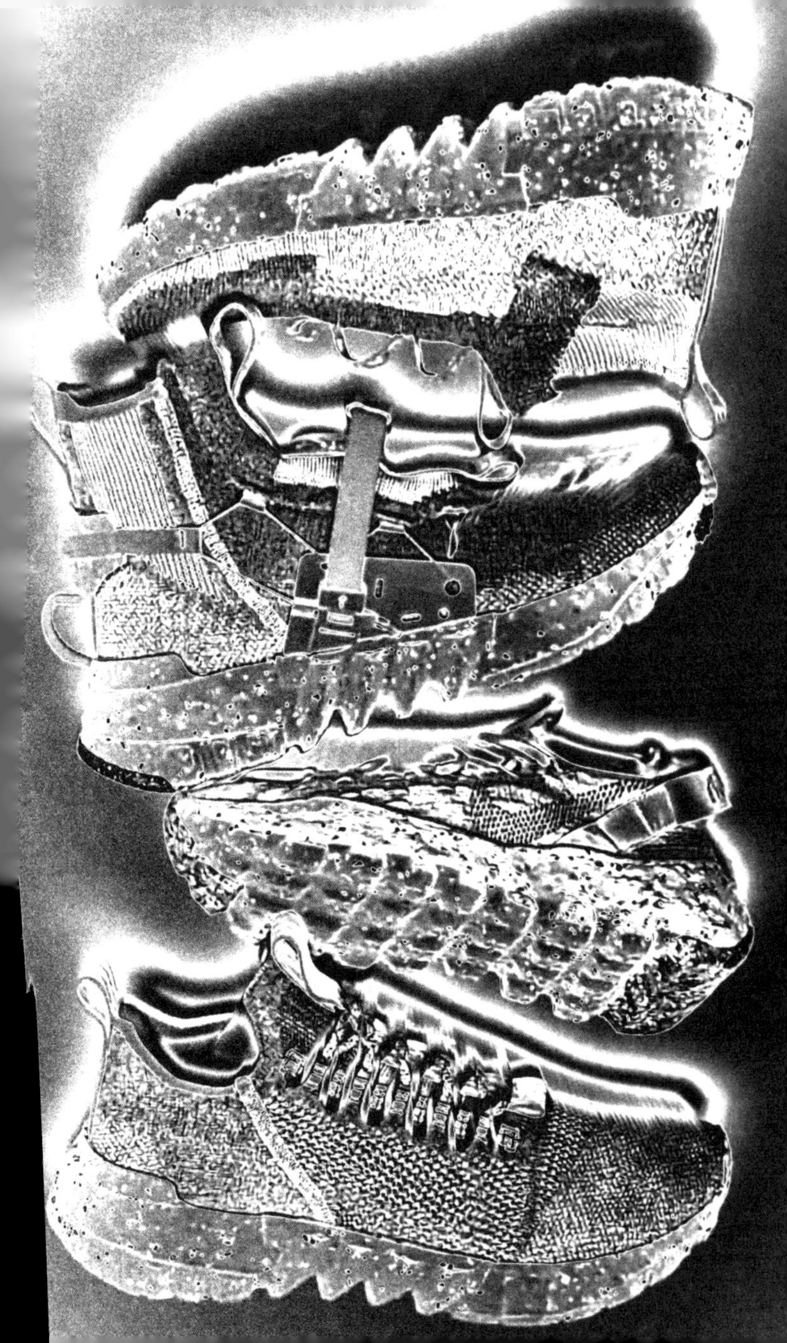

But recycling gets complicated when you start making bicomponent and tricomponent materials. The ability to recover individual elements or return those materials to a state where they can become the building blocks for new products almost completely disappears. For this reason, recycling within the context of fossil fuel-based materials has traditionally been a game of diminishing returns. Material quality and performance degrade with each new use.

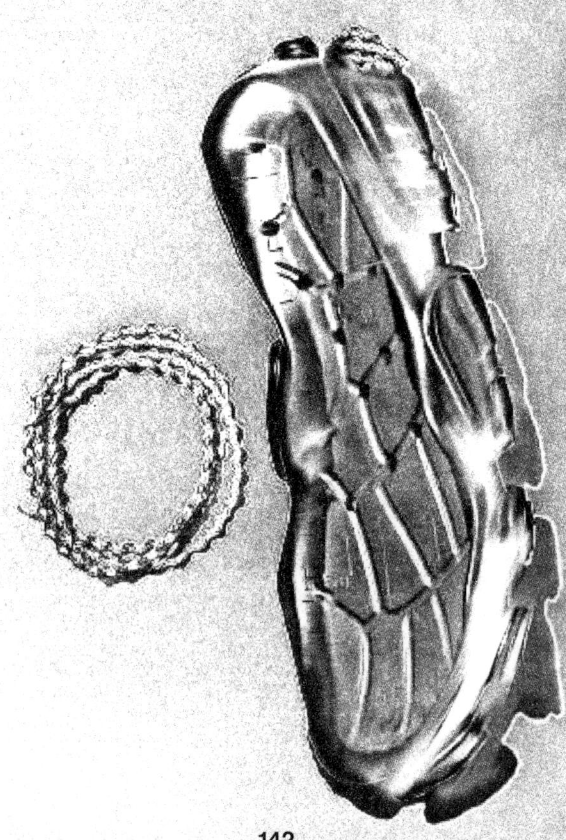

With this in mind, Nike's design criteria have already expanded beyond traditional factors like performance, durability, and aesthetics to add end-of-life and disassembly as key considerations. The ISPA Link Axis demonstrates how avant-garde designs can emerge from incorporating these considerations at the front end of the design process. The shoe is not only made largely from recycled materials; it also comes apart into just four pieces, with a cleverly interlocking recycled polyester Flyknit upper and TPU outsole.

Even with such advances, teams looking further ahead didn't have to look too far for more examples.

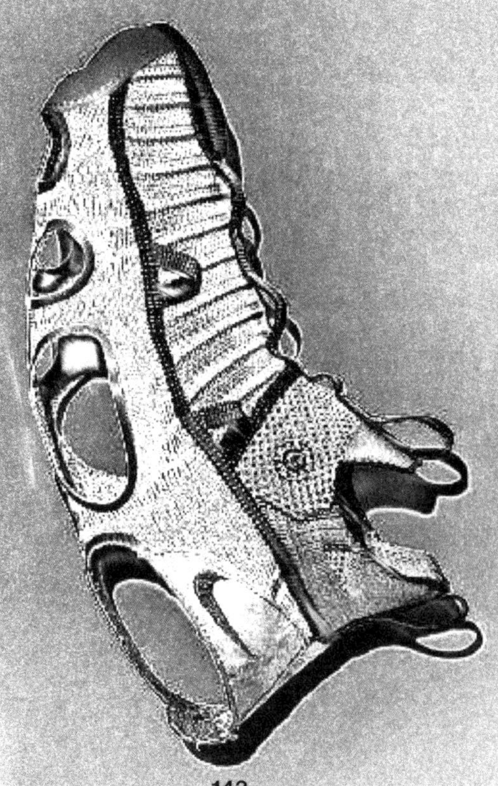

Mother Nature is the ultimate recycler.

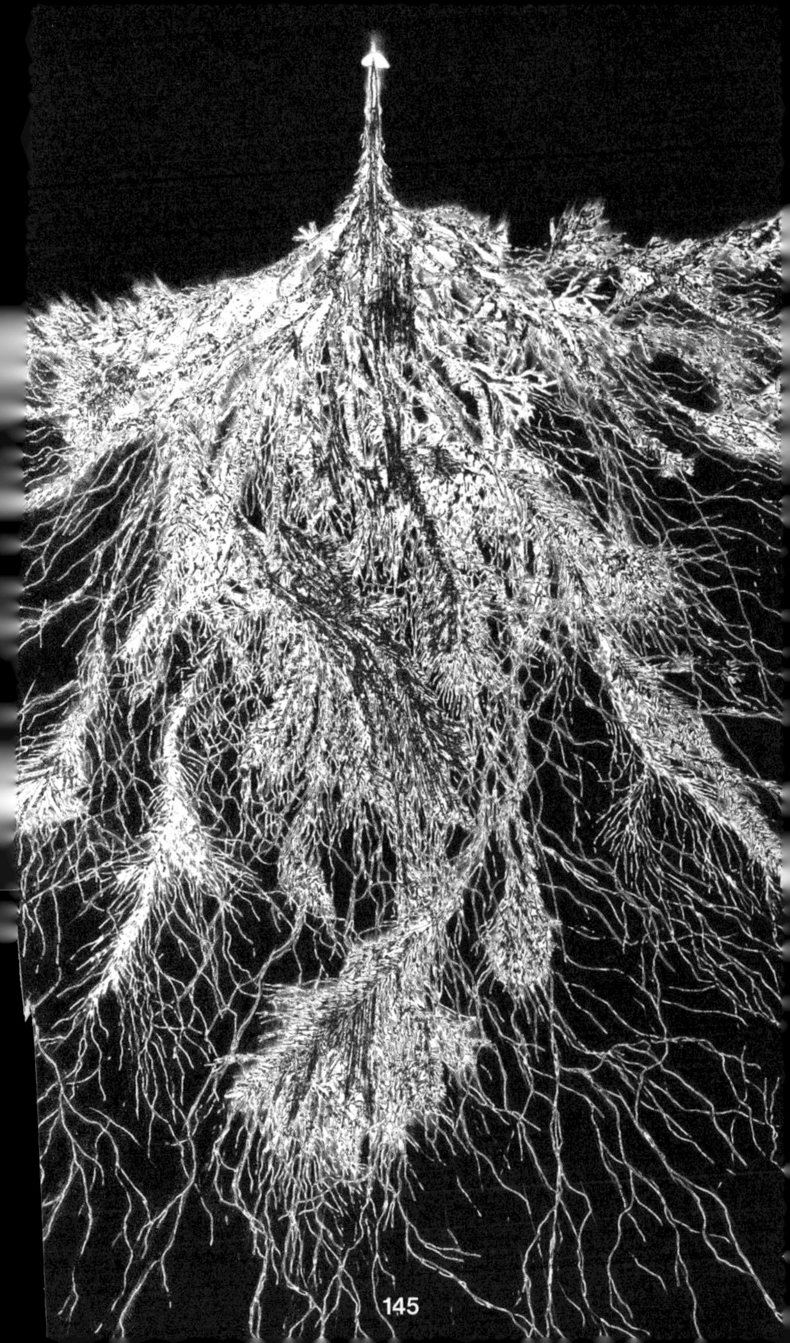

From biological digestion to self-healing cellular structures, the natural world offers an incredible array of blueprints to feed the next generation of innovation at Nike. If the cultivated plant-based "meats" and cell-grown salmon fillets in your grocery aisle demonstrate anything, biomaterials designed to harness and work with the time-tested processes inherent to life on Earth will increasingly factor into life in the 21st century.

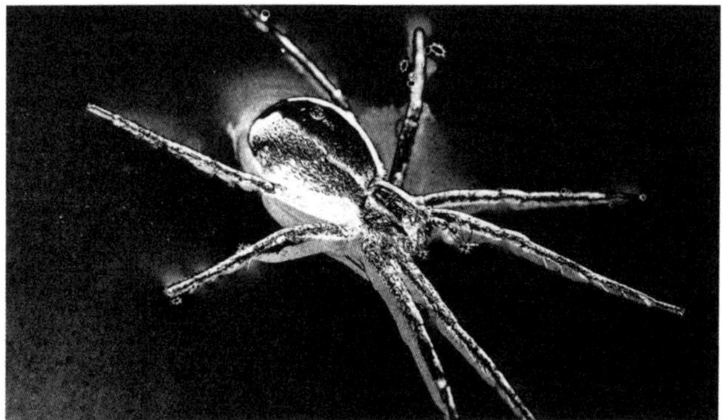

Further afield, scientists are working on growing complex tissues and organs like eyes, tear ducts, and even a miniature brain. For Nike's part, the company continues to explore and scale alternative lower-carbon materials derived from the natural world and, in the case of Nike Forward, of its own making.

While most design today happens at a structural level, as we further utilize nature's properties and processes and connect them to design platforms empowered by machine learning and A.I., design will increasingly happen at a molecular, even subatomic, level. Somewhere down the line, it's not too outlandish to consider an entire garment or pair of shoes being grown instead of pieced together.

Carbon capture represents yet another potentially game-changing category of materials Nike is investigating. It offers ways to take pollutants from other industries like steel production and safely embed them into polymers that can be used in any number of ways.

Nike recently announced a partnership with Newlight Technologies, a California-based firm that's figured out how to make a carbon-negative plastic-like material with an ocean-based microorganism that eats methane or carbon dioxide and turns it into the molecule polyhydroxybutyrate, which can be harvested and melted down into a useful polymer. By fully harnessing materials like this, Nike may be able to create products that completely upend our current sustainability paradigm. While we inherently assume that more stuff means more bad in the world, when you make a net-negative-carbon product, that's no longer true.

That's a radical difference in the way we think about what it means to be a consumer and a designer, and it's exactly the kind of paradigm shift Nike is directing its innovation and design initiatives toward. There's no reason that sustainable or circular products can't be joyful, delighting users by subverting their expectations or by providing a solution that at one time would have been completely unthinkable. This isn't simply about making better materials and products; it's about impacting the entire organizational ecosystem within Nike, the broader worlds of sport and fashion, and, ultimately, the athletes and communities who intersect with the Swoosh.

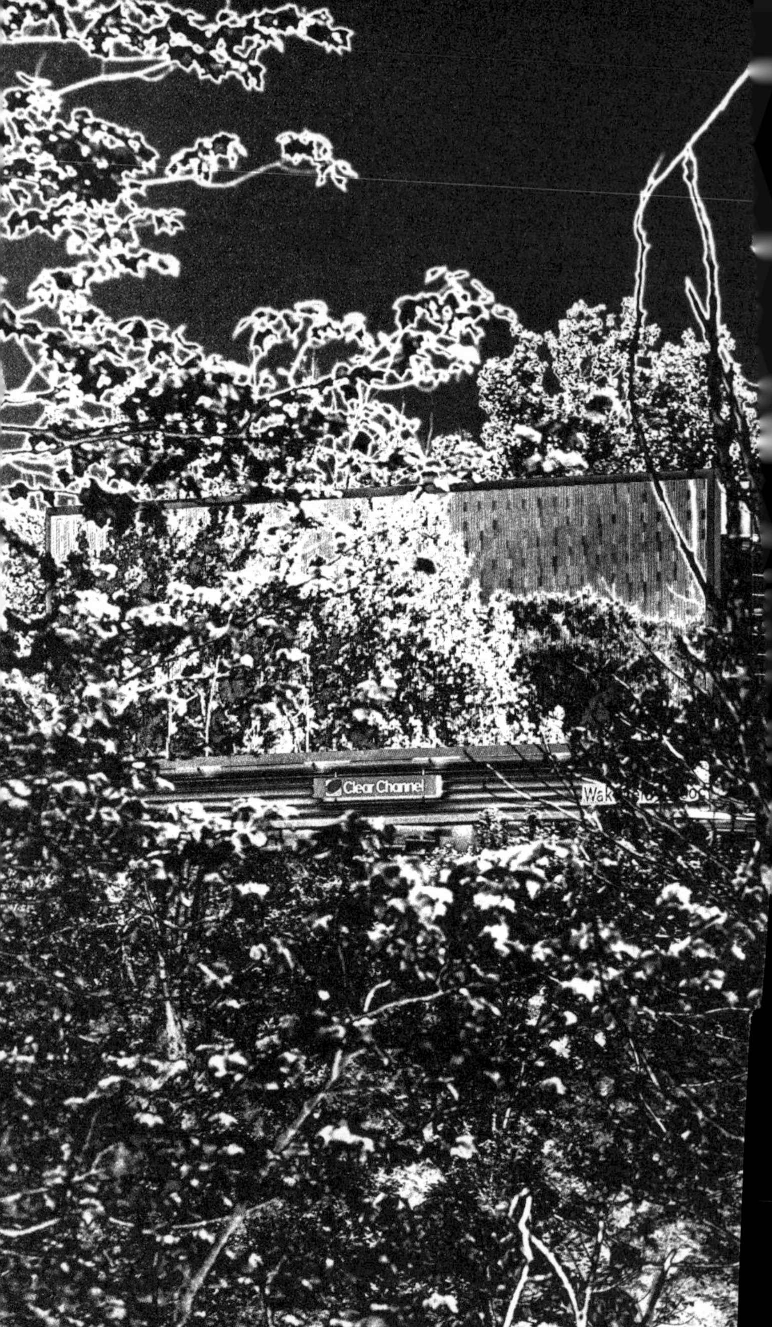
Clear Channel

To do so will require a multiplicity of solutions — a mosaic of recycled content, biomaterials, and carbon capture. There's no one thing anyone can swap in for fossil fuels that can serve all the needs Nike has and foresees. And while that challenge is not insignificant, it's also representative of the kind of problem-solving designers love to tackle head-on.

Some of the difficulty is that these things are now achievable (like mushroom leather), or on the cusp of possibility (like gasifying old product to return it to a useable raw state), but not at scale. The work then becomes about charting the path of how to get there, setting bolts on the climbing wall for future generations to follow and build on.

The entire effort starts with simply doing less bad: drawing down carbon, subbing in alternative materials and approaches, incorporating innovations from other industries, and building more connections with communities outside of Nike to create a stronger web of influence and resilience. To get to a functioning vision of circularity will require forging new habits on an unprecedented scale.

Across each of the defined zones (industrial, consumer, and post-consumer), changing attitudes and behaviors will be as, if not more, important than the physical stuff. Symbiosis is defined as "interaction between two different organisms living in close physical association, typically to the advantage of both." For Nike, it means building systems that enable a variety of living, mutually beneficial relationships with athletes, ecosystems, suppliers, makers, industries, and even competitors.

There is no "winning" at making the planet healthier and more habitable.

We're all in it together.

This essential truth necessitates thinking beyond tangible product to redefine what true value is. Value, in the context of symbiosis, is contributing to the well-being and good health of larger systems, creating new opportunities for connection, learning, equity, and growth. It could even mean actively giving back and repairing more than taking or extracting. It's folly to think we can master nature, but unless we do more to work within its bounds, it will master us.

To that end, Carl Sagan offered this sage wisdom in 1994: "Our planet is a lonely speck in the great enveloping cosmic dark. In our obscurity, in all this vastness, there is no hint that help will come from elsewhere to save us from ourselves." Instead of waiting for help from elsewhere, Nike is moving toward new pathways for broader contribution and collaboration. Ultimately,

MARCH

$1

Whole Earth Catalog

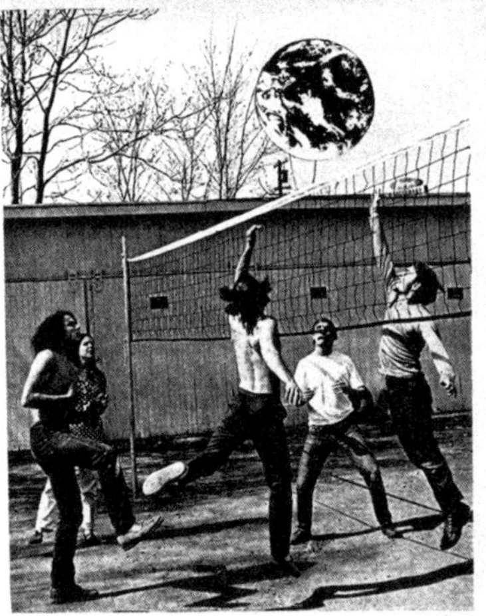

THE WORLD GAME

"I travel around the world a great deal, and everywhere I hear humanity saying, 'We are not against any other human beings; we feel the world ought to work properly.' Everywhere they say it's our politicians that get us into trouble. This is the majority viewpoint all around the earth today."

—R. Buckminster Fuller

See page 30

there's just

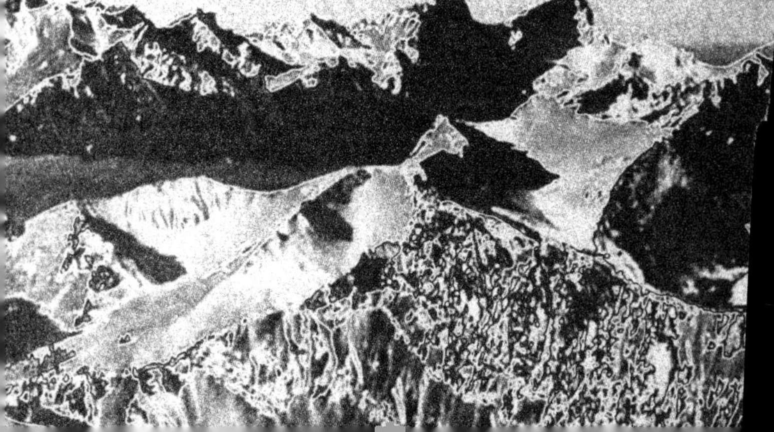

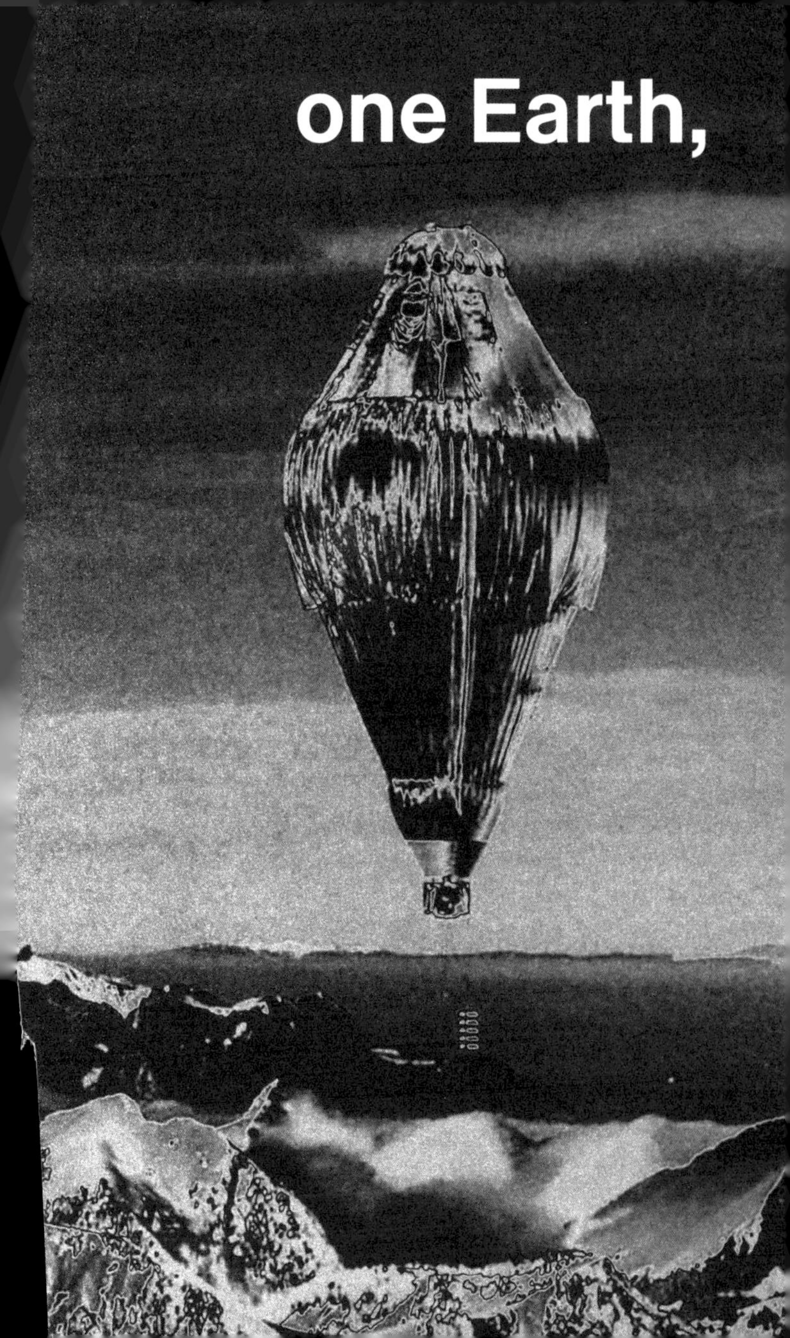
one Earth,

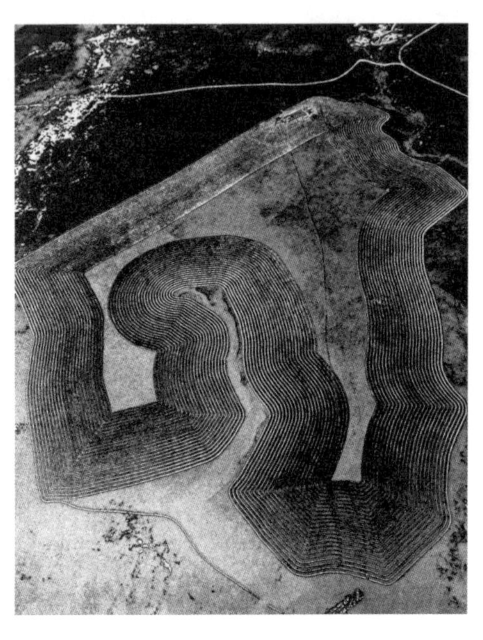

and it's the only playground we've got.

Cabinet of Wonders

The first thing the design students saw as they exited the elevator onto the 17th floor of a Manhattan high-rise was an enormous aquarium. Color-shifting sea creatures drifted behind thick glass, looping past one another in lazy gyres before disappearing into forests of kelp. An octopus flashed by, then another; they seemed to be playing.

Lurking in the center of all the water was a reef unlike anything the students had seen before: angular, abstract, constructed from modular blocks. As they stared at an unusual object growing from a thick branch of coral, a diver floated into view, collecting samples.

Their host, Alessandro, cleared his throat. "Amazing, right?" he said. He and the teacher shook hands. Alessandro noticed the students' attention was still on the diver, who was scraping some sort of resin from part of the reef. "That's our marine biophysicist. She's taking samples. See, the reef, it's a manufacturing system. We're producing coatings, gels, resins, dyes—"

As if on cue, an octopus emitted a burst of brightly colored ink that settled down across the reef like an abstract painting.

"Those shells you see—the coral, those rocks, all that sand—are *grown*. It's artificial, in a sense, but it's living. Organic. And this is just a demonstration. I mean, we are in Midtown Manhattan!" The students were in awe. "We have reefs co-creating materials all over the world: Indonesia, Australia, even Oregon."

The students had been expecting something very different from a visit to Nike's vaunted materials archive, built in the very heart of New York City. They thought they'd be handling the jerseys of legendary athletes or looking at prototypes of shoes mounted like museum displays. But the sequence of rooms they were about to enter felt more like a natural history museum, an object library hosting exotic materials meant to inspire athletes and designers alike.

The walls of the next room were lined with beautiful glass cases holding seashells sitting beside engineered gelatins, which shared shelf space with synthetic minerals, animal horns, biodegradable plastics, and spun fibers woven from rainforest vines. In a case at least 10 feet tall, a bioluminescent spider web glimmered in its own emitted light.

The students started fanning out, amazed by the range of objects and materials, but Alessandro asked them to come back and gather round. He picked up a bird feather. Everything in the room, he explained, was a material that Nike's design labs were now working with: clothing from spider silk; sports equipment from lunar metals; inlays, molecular adhesives, new foams, and volcanic glass compounds.

"Feel free to touch stuff," he urged. "You'll recognize some of it. A lot of this is in those shoes and T-shirts you're wearing. Go ahead."

One student ran her palm along a perfectly black crystal the size of a soccer ball and recoiled. It was *warm*. She had no idea what the material was.

Alessandro grinned. "That, what you're touching, was also grown. We use it in performance sensors. The stuff you're seeing here, it's not just games and sports. It can be used in medical equipment, responsive materials, and diagnostic tools."

He turned back to the group and urged them onward to the next room. It was the size of a basketball court but designed like a planetarium. The ceiling lights were in the patterns of constellations, shining down to illuminate Martian rocks and chunks of lunar minerals.

"Imagine, next season," said Alessandro, "a football made from stardust, or a bat made from metal harvested in space." In one hand he still held the bird feather as he picked up a clunky, sealed container; inside were particles harvested from a comet's tail. He showed everyone a shimmering textile milled in Nike's zero-gravity weaving labs. A few students reached forward to touch it; it felt like water.

"If you remember anything from your visit today," continued Alessandro, "make it this: you can learn as much from a piece of bark or a dove's feather as you can from carbon fiber or titanium. A rock from Mars has as many design possibilities as an athlete's favorite material. Learn to design *with* the world, and you'll see that nature's already done half the job for you."

A quiet student near the edge of the room, he noticed, was sketching something on her tablet. He walked over and looked. She had drawn hummingbird wings made from paper-thin sheets of woven metal, which she then extended with a few elegant lines that became the folds of a new garment. She sketched the garment unthreading outward into planets and stars.

"It looks like you're getting the hang of it," he said, before ushering them all into the next room.

Static to Sensorial

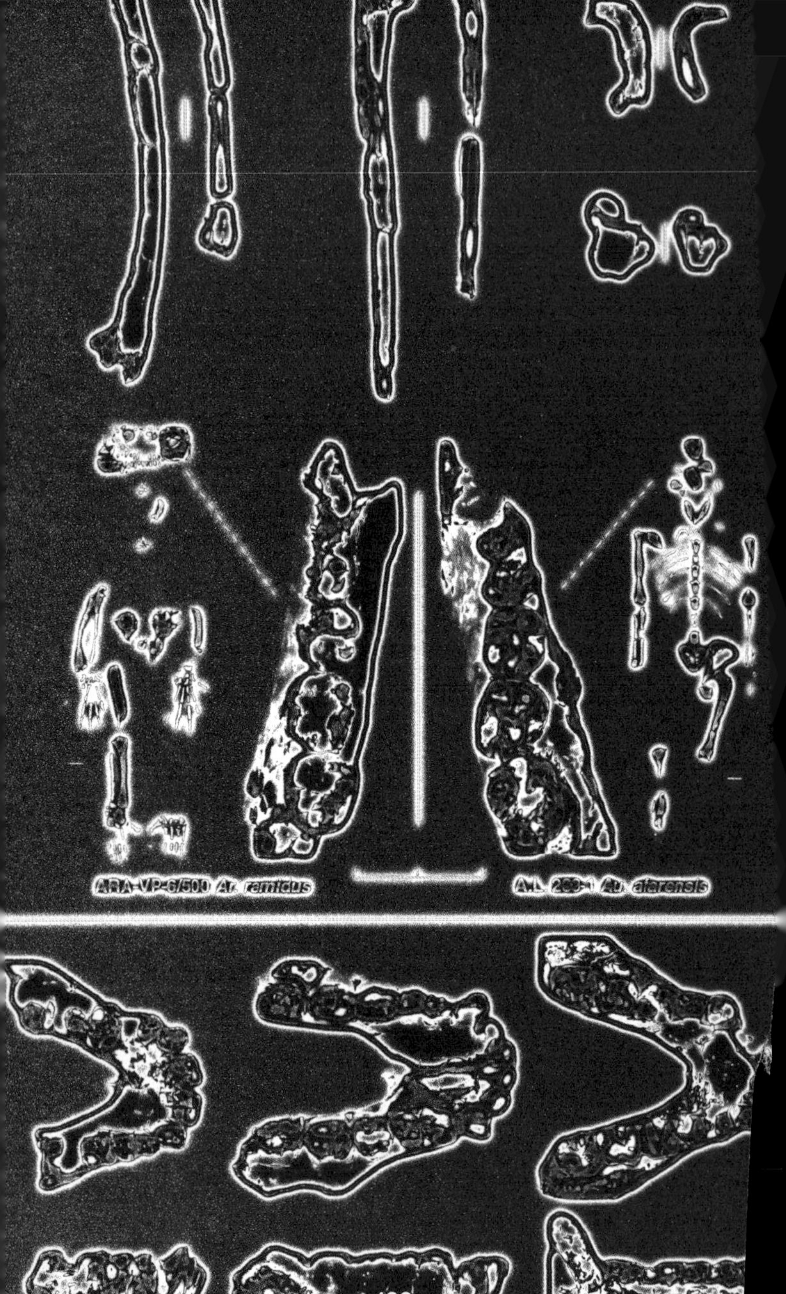
ARA-VP-6/500 Ar. ramidus
A.L. 288-1 Au. afarensis

Radiometric data informs us that the Earth is 4.5 billion years old. One of the oldest tangible links to human ancestors, a primate group called *Ardipithecus*, began walking upright some 6 million years ago, a period that represents a mere 0.13 percent of the planet's history.

Our species, *Homo sapiens*, emerged some 300,000 years ago and, for about the next 290,000 years, spread over the continents as disparate tribes of hunter-gatherers. It was only in the last 10,000 years that humans developed agriculture, written language, and metal tools and organized themselves into the cultures, states, and cities that fill our history books. And 200 years ago, in what amounts to just 0.06 percent of human history, the Industrial Revolution ushered in another crucial turning point for humanity as the mechanized production of goods, increased implementation of scientific research and principles, and global trade began to form the world as we know it today.

While it seems astonishing that so much of human progress has transpired in such a relatively condensed window, the changes on our doorstep may be even more profound. Although the advancement of mechanical technology has seemingly eased in recent decades (after all, most of our cars and planes are not drastically different from those of the 1960s), the exponential and explosive evolution of digital technology has more than made up the difference.

Tech now permeates and mediates almost every aspect of our lives, including communication channels, physical infrastructure, economic markets, healthcare, education, and energy production. And while this may not seem entirely new, the connectivity between 8 billion humans and their devices and computers, as well as the data and intelligence produced through these interactions, has reached a magnitude that is drastically reshaping life as we know it.

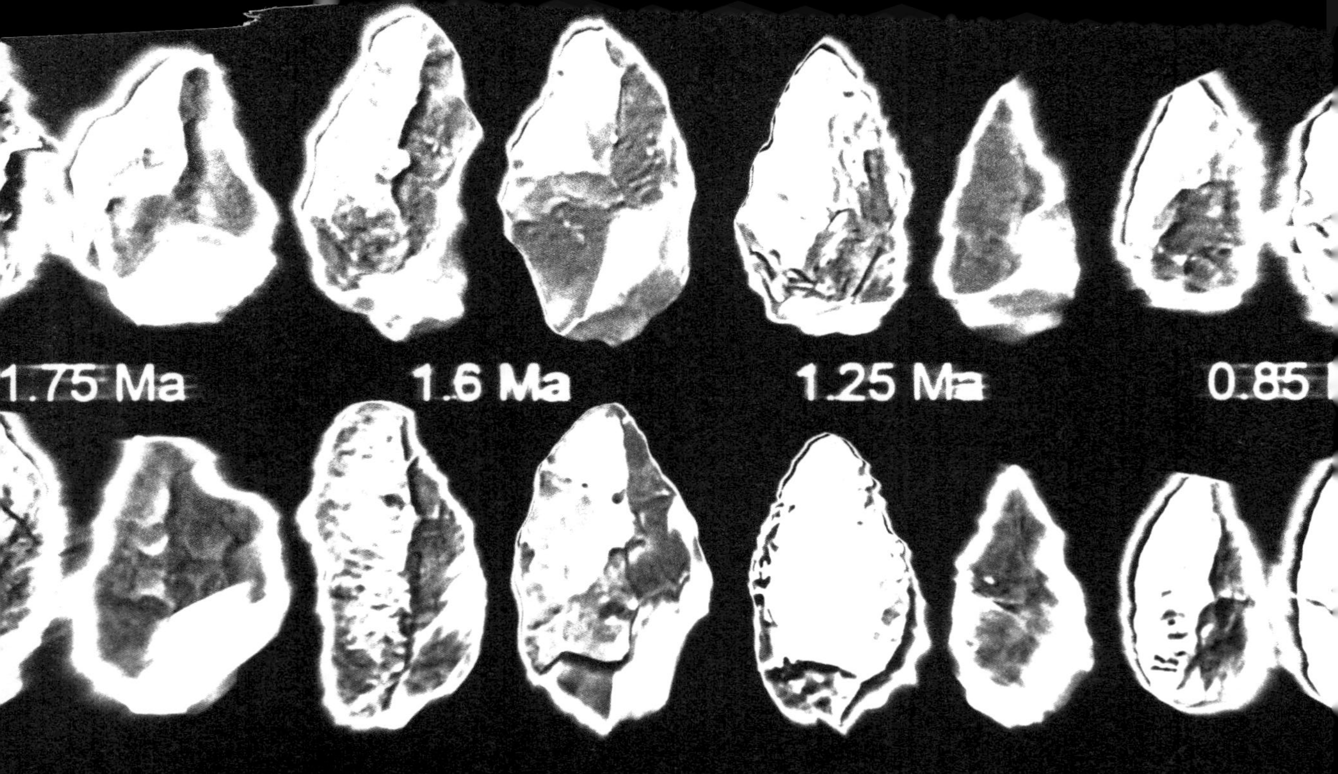
1.75 Ma
1.6 Ma
1.25 Ma
0.85

As a leading indication of this transformation — from a purely statistical point of view — there is as much digital information being created by humans today as there is biological information in the biosphere.

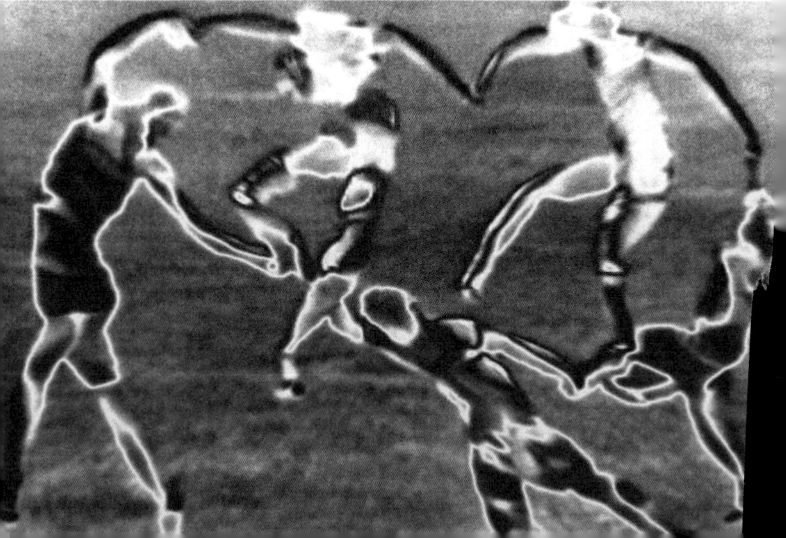

In the years ahead, as connected devices (the so-called Internet of Things) continue to proliferate, computer-processing power escalates exponentially, robotics become more commonplace, and artificial intelligence and machine-learning algorithms are invariably applied to walks of life that once seemed immune from technological intervention, humans may well face something akin to an evolutionary transition, where biology, society, and technology synthesize in ways that would have seemed unimaginable a few short decades ago.

it used to be that things had computers in them

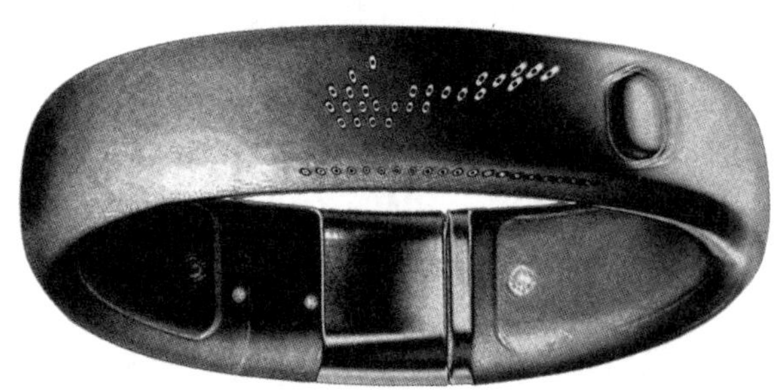

now they are computers with things attached to them

Within these broader societal and technological transitions, Nike is adapting as well. While the company already runs on a significant digital infrastructure, Nike recognizes the fundamental role that technology will play across the board going forward. Or, as the technologist Bruce Schneier wrote, "It used to be that things had computers in them. Now they are computers with things attached to them."

Although we don't yet wear computers on our feet, the company put semiconductors and microchips into Nike+ footwear as far back as 2006, pioneered the wearables market at the dawn of the new millennium with one of the earliest MP3 players and products like FuelBand, started to build a connected community through networked smartphone apps for running and fitness, and has — through the Adapt line — begun to make inroads to a product that senses and responds by tightening and loosening its laces. But while this foundation is being laid, the cutting edge of innovation promises to integrate a level of intelligence, connectivity, and equity into future products that will make these efforts look neolithic by comparison.

Creating within this new landscape will require new kinds of designers who will be as fluent in programming lines of code and developing algorithms as they are in 3D modeling or rotational molding. When a product becomes part of a connected ecosystem, that means we're no longer just talking about product design. We're building entire worlds around those products and experiences that are inclusive and accessible to all.

For Nike to create authentic and operable worlds where products and people seamlessly connect, it will require new fields and roles that intersect with design. It will take psychologists collaborating with colorists, chemical engineers finding solutions with architects, and machine-learning specialists teaming up with weavers.

To great effect, this kind of fusion has already empowered a generation of design at Nike— and it's no secret that real innovation occurs when differing areas of knowledge are meaningfully brought into contact with one another. Progress, and the acceleration of progress, arise from exactly these kinds of circumstances and collisions.

inclusive and accessible to all

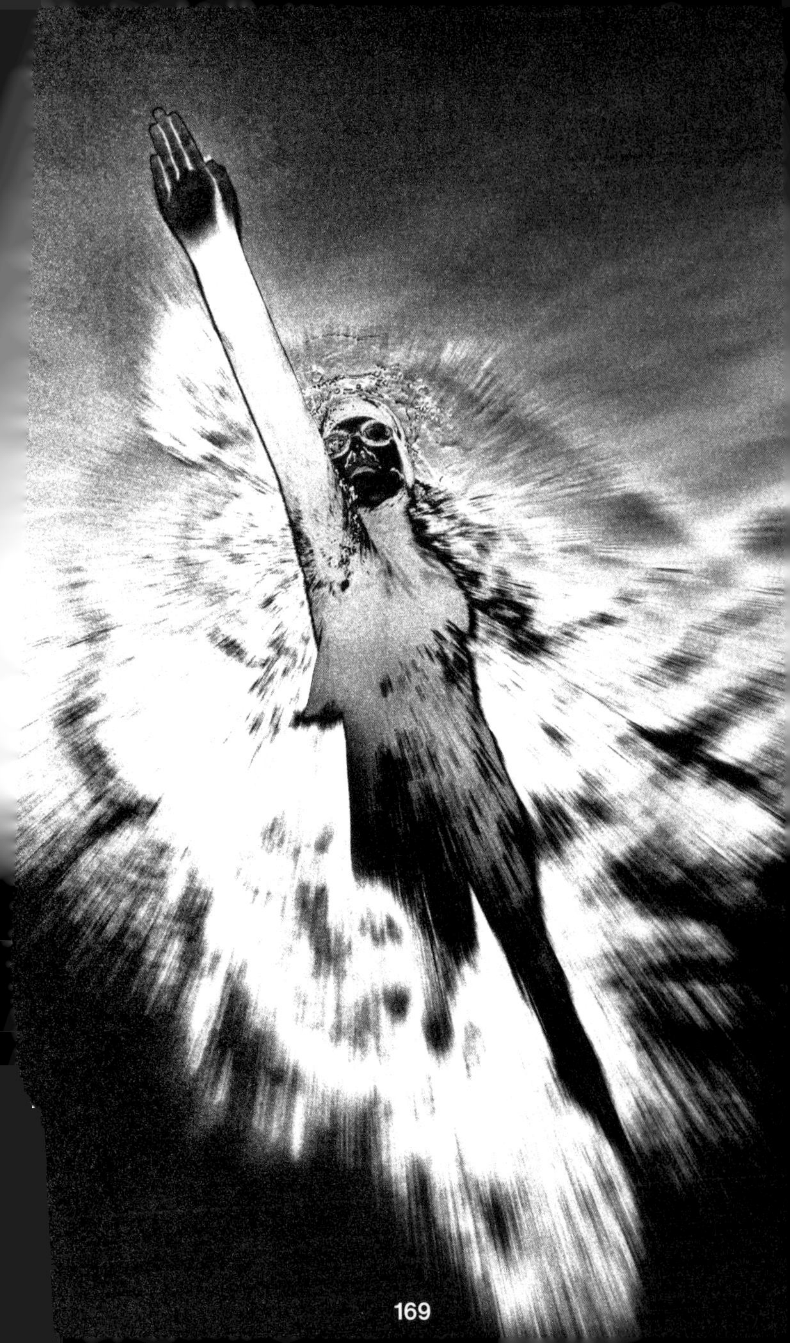

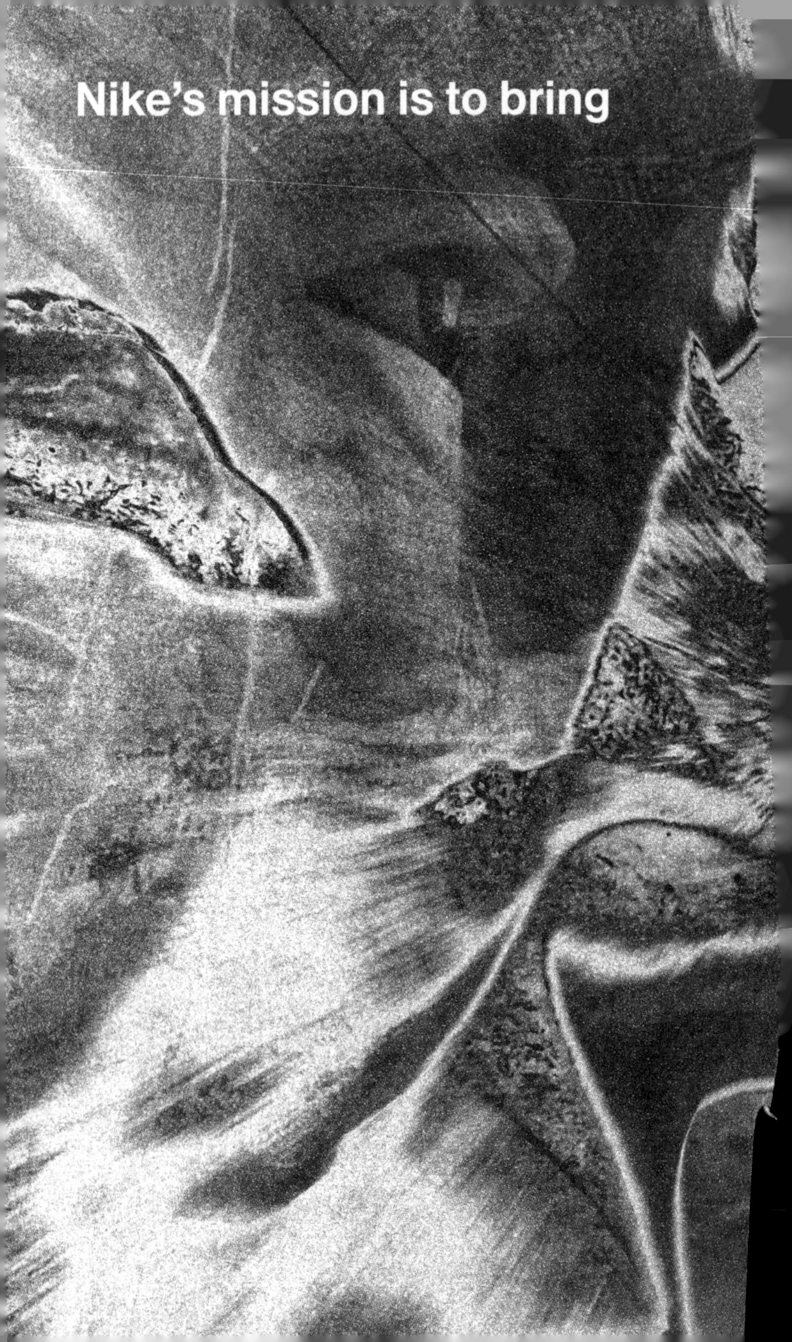
Nike's mission is to bring

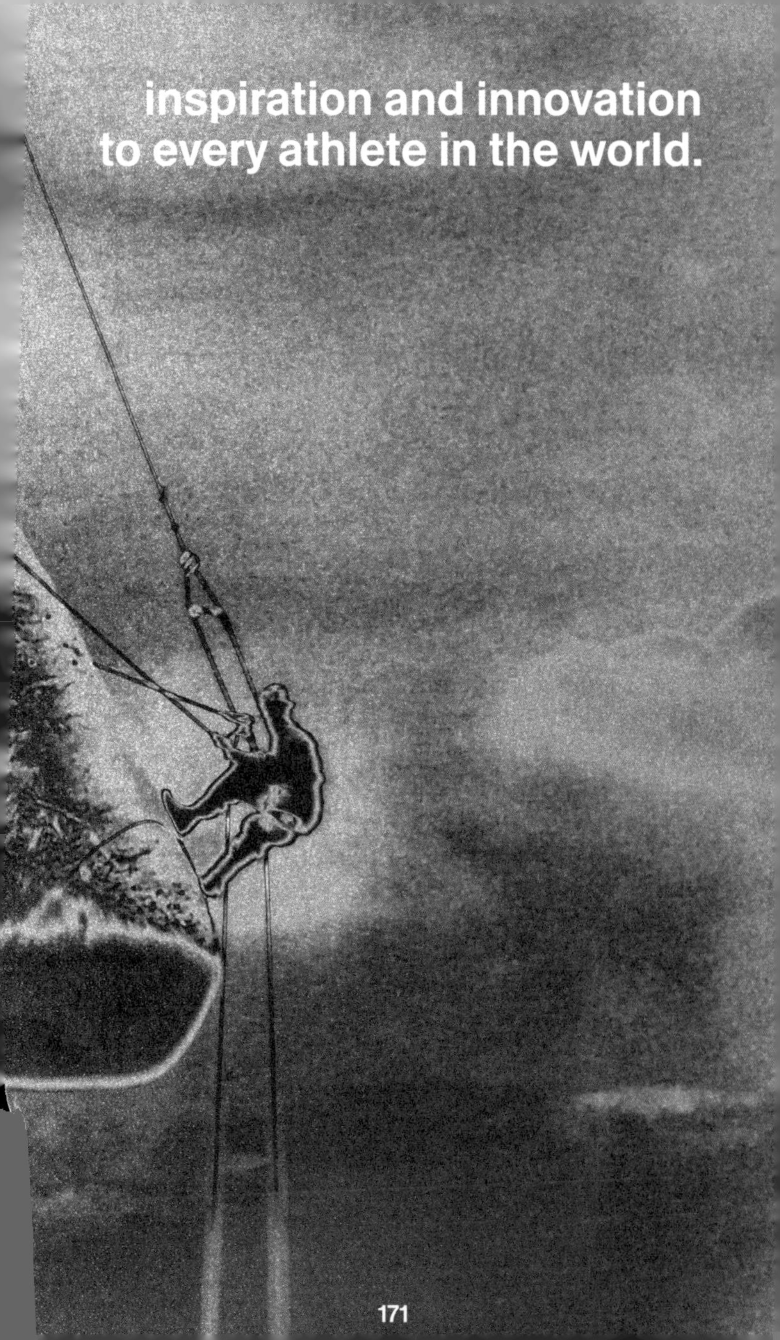

inspiration and innovation
to every athlete in the world.

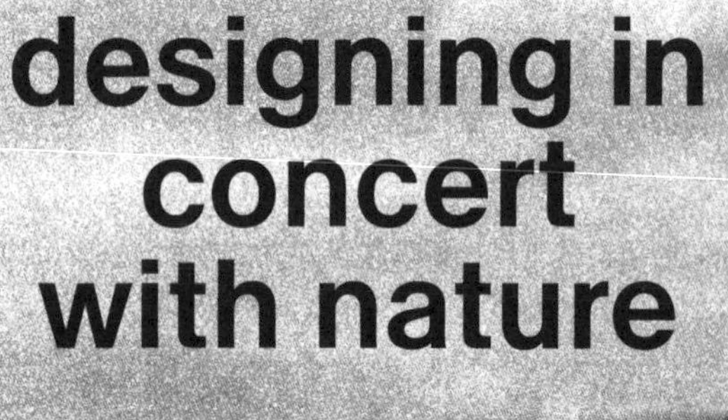
designing in
concert
with nature

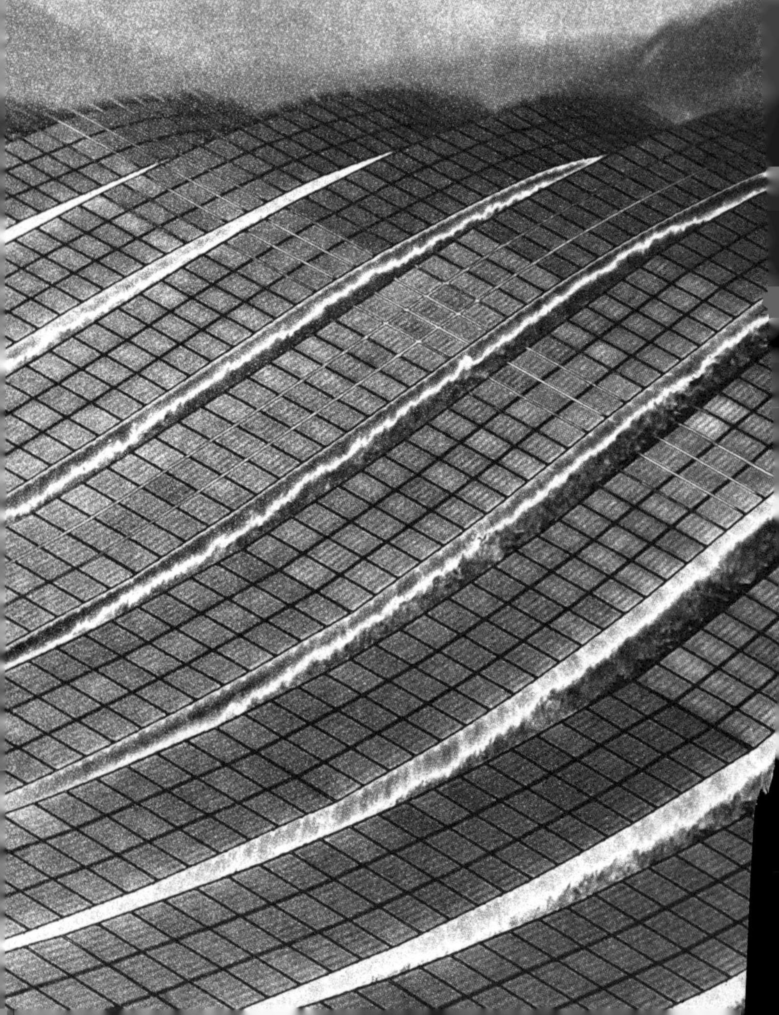

The company isn't making the effort to embed sensors into products like footwear and apparel and build the infrastructures and ecosystems to process and interpret all that data just because it's the next big thing, but rather to deliver more meaningful experiences of sport to more athletes. And for Nike, that means designing for the world's most elite athletes at the peak of their game as well as for anyone who identifies as an athlete physically, psychologically, intellectually, emotionally, or spiritually. That also means embracing the diversity and intersectionality of athletes' experiences, identities, strengths, and disabilities.

The themes swirling through Nike's corridors and creative teams — like expansive creative platforms, enhanced personalization, seamless motivation, inclusivity, and designing in concert with nature — all coalesce through these future-facing endeavors, or what might be termed "intelligent augmentation." For the skeptics and purists who dismiss the role a soft goods-producing sportswear and footwear company can play in this field, consider that Nike's product has always been a form of augmentation.

Shoes not only protect our feet and ankles but also supplement our ability to run faster and jump higher. Adding a layer of intelligence to these products so that they can sense and respond in real time is, in effect, not dissimilar from adding improved cushioning or solving for a greater range of motion and access. It's just pushing what already exists into a different, more inclusive, and technologically enhanced vector.

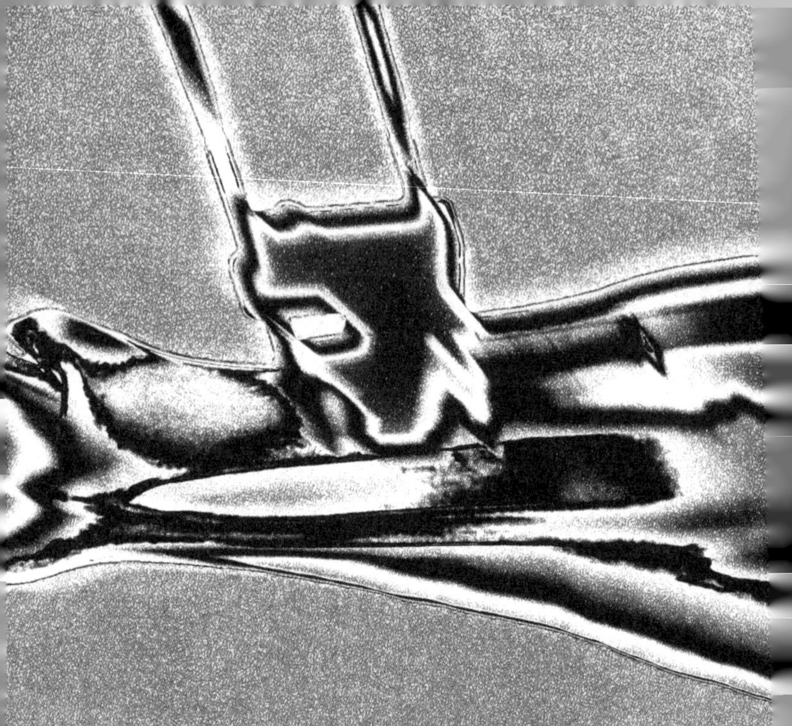

Through a certain lens, human augmentation is as old as the earliest hand tools, the basic stone implements made by our ancestors some 2.6 million years ago. Our capacity to predetermine a cause and effect and extend our abilities beyond what our physical bodies can

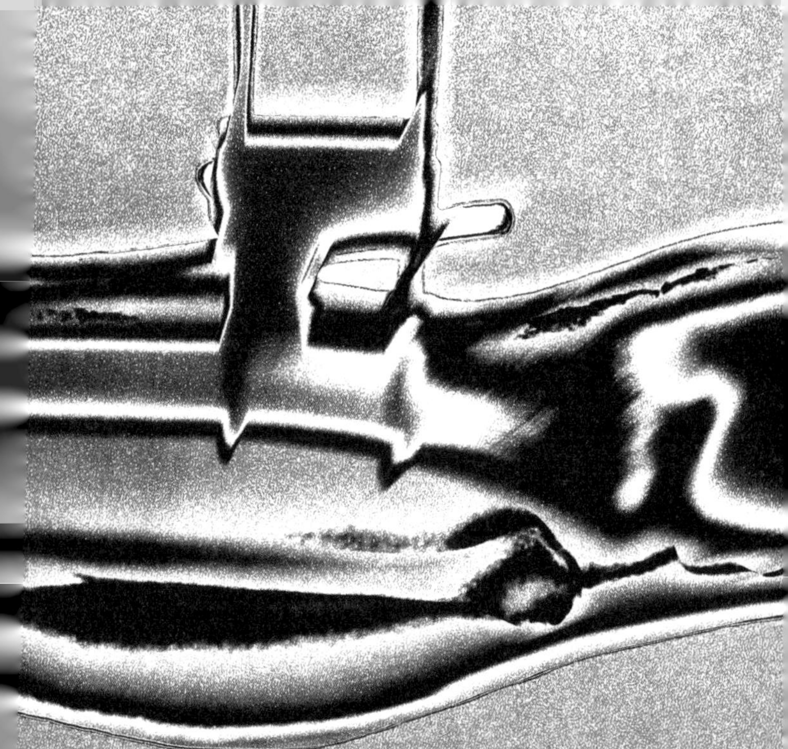

accomplish has enabled us to modify the environment and extend our lives. Although the toolset has changed immensely, the basic premise has not: the purpose of augmentation is to simulate, assist, adapt, supplement, elevate, and exceed human abilities and disabilities.

Augmentation can offer a means of simulating a function that a person may not be able to perform permanently, temporarily, or situationally. Prosthetics, cochlear implants, and hearing aids are probably the most typical and ubiquitous examples of assistive technologies that help people with disabilities participate in society and be independent. At the leading edge of where augmentation for simulation is headed, researchers have figured out how to tap faint, latent signals from arm nerves and amplify them. This enables real-time, intuitive finger-level control of bionic limbs, leading to ultra-precise mind-controlled prosthetics for individuals with an amputation.

Supplementing human ability takes simulation one step further by enabling different people to do things that are already possible, but better: running faster, jumping higher, or lifting heavier things. Boosting our strength, speed, endurance, and senses would redefine the human experience in fundamental ways that are of immense interest to a company dedicated to helping people with and without disabilities maximize their potential through movement and sport.

With innovations like HyperAdapt, Nike is already exploring what it means to develop products that supplement our somatic experience of sport and extend the physicality of the human body. The shoe famously started as the self-lacing high-top in 1989's *Back to the Future Part II*. But as it became a reality in 2015, teams at Nike realized that the squeezing motion of the mechanism also offered a vehicle for communication to the wearer, a kind of Morse code for the body (or, as one Nike designer dubbed it, "skin-top computing"). Right now, that alphabet consists of just two letters, tight and loose.

But as these technologies develop, they could expand to include an entire sensory vocabulary (soft/hard, slow/fast) and respond to a variety of conditions.

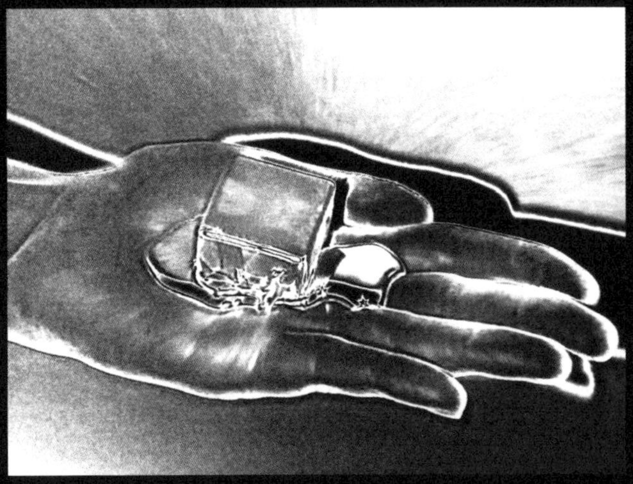

Given the rate of technological change, certain science fictions could soon become science realities: flying, invisibility, self-repairing tissues, underwater breathing, and synthetic memory are all possibilities in the earliest stages of development. As Nike considers what that future may look like, its designers and innovators are pondering how to unlock new senses and experiences as we retrain ourselves for an entirely new definition of sport. What if Nike could infuse their products with

the smell of victory

the feeling of draining a buzzer-beating three-pointer

the smell of victory, embed the seamless synchronization of a school of fish or the murmuration of birds in flight to its football kits, or deliver the feeling of draining a buzzer-beating three-pointer to everyone watching a championship game?

As teams situated at the furthest reaches of Nike innovation contemplate the road map to get to that future, they see the technology of batteries, motors, and actuators improving. But there's still a long way to go to put the pieces together — and do it in such a way that people with different bodies and different needs will feel included and invite the interaction.

It's one thing to use a piece of equipment like a bike or scooter, or a device that you can stash in your pocket or wear on your wrist. It's another thing entirely to design for symbiosis with the human body in motion. Everyone moves slightly differently. Our bodies are asymmetrical and disproportionate. Designing for such a range of body types and biomechanical processes is a vastly tougher assignment.

Inviting such technology to be a part of our persona also has psychological and emotional implications. Unlike hardware that sits on a table, we choose what we wear based on how it feels and functions in contact with our skin and bodies, if it makes us look and feel good, or whether it's socially or culturally appropriate in a variety of contexts.

Another consideration is, if it's the only garment in your entire wardrobe that offers such functionality, how likely are you to wear it or make use of the tech often? The inherent complexity of the problems that require solving in this arena are enough to stymie even the most advanced innovation teams, because ultimately, for the solution not

to be rejected out of hand, it must be frictionless for the user. It has to produce a "wow" right out of the box or off the hanger.

As far out as these concepts get, Nike's North Star is fixed on championing athletes and sport. So each step toward the unknown is weighed against whether it will help us stay human and further our humanity, whether performing epic athletic feats or simply showing up each day. The aim of creating intelligent and inclusive products that can sense and respond isn't to exert control. It's to help more people feel more empowered, embodied, and connected — to themselves, to the human experience, and to each other.

In his classic 1933 essay on aesthetics, "In Praise of Shadows," Junichiro Tanizaki wrote,

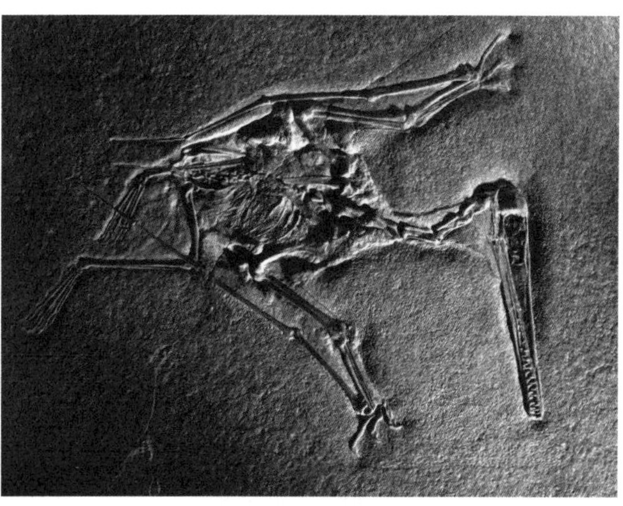

"The older we get the more we seem to think that everything was better in the past... Never has there been an age that people have been satisfied with."

This is undoubtedly true: every human life has transpired within the context of constant change.

It's more comforting to imagine living within the warm embrace of what we already know to be true than what we can't yet understand or foresee. But paradoxically, our dissatisfaction with the present is also what drives us forward. It becomes the catalyst for design — a desire to shape a better world in which to live. While there is uncertainty and no shortage of challenges ahead, it's somehow heartening to remind ourselves that this is simply what humans do.

For millennia, humankind has been forced to reckon with the idea that nothing is constant. Design, as a human activity, is a means of negotiating the unpredictability of the present. And to design, we must have some sense of what we intend to do, of where things will go, of what investment of time and resources will have the most profound impact on our goals.

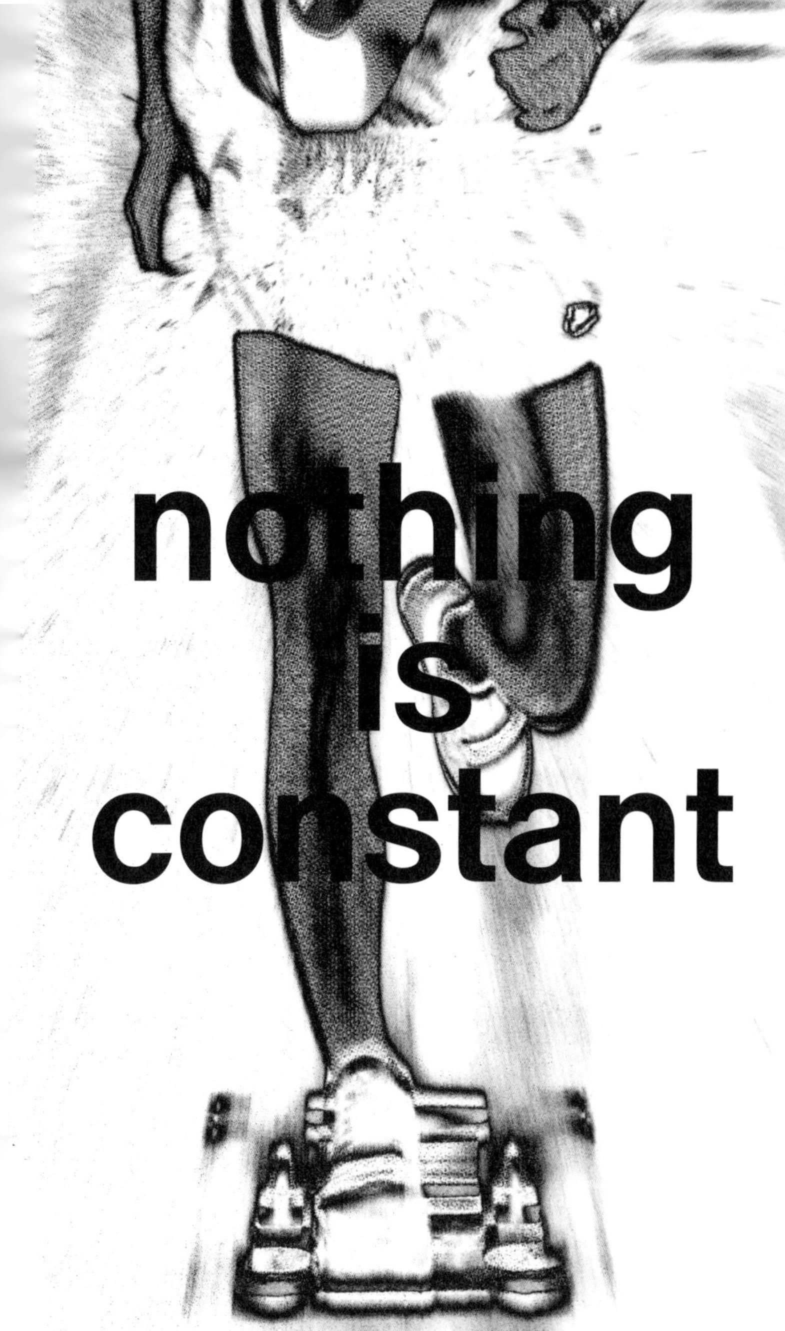
nothing
is
constant

For Nike, that means the next great leap in innovation is as likely to come from a daisy as it is from a waffle iron.

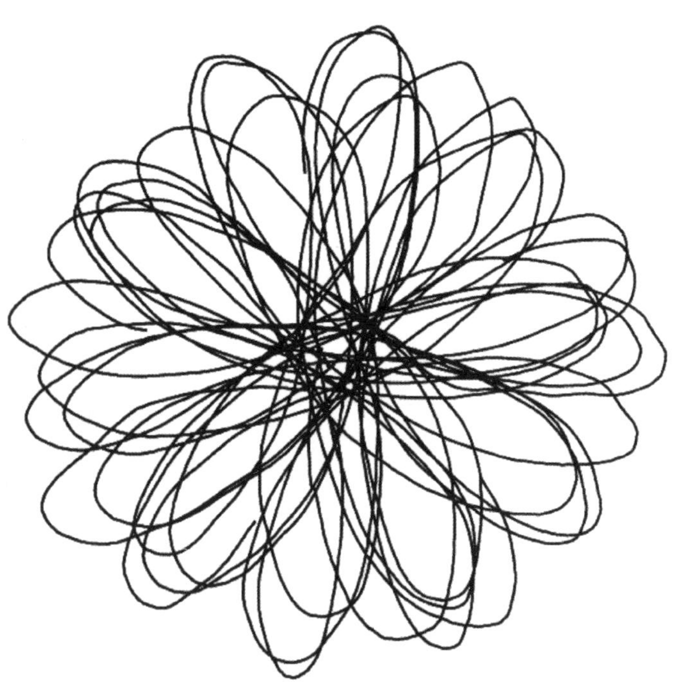

Winterplex

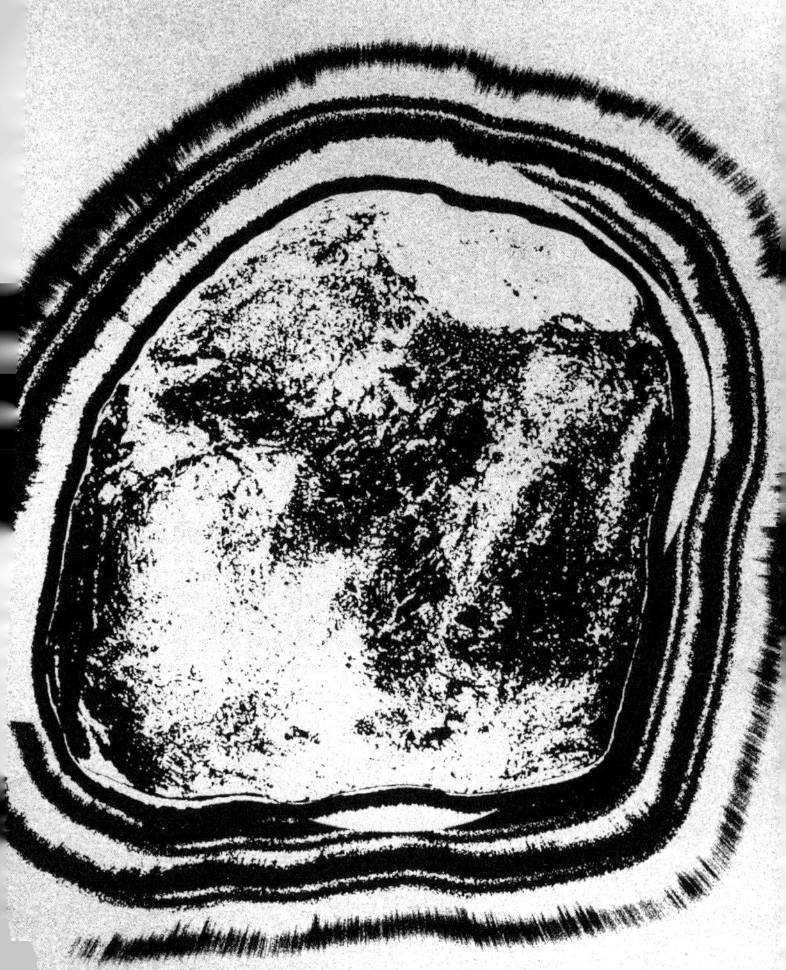

When the warehouse door slid open, the technician, Taylor, quietly laughed. The snow inside was much deeper than expected. "The equipment must be a little hyperactive today," he said to his guest. "But that's good. We'll see the complex in full effect."

The two of them were about to enter Nike's huge new facility for testing winter sports gear, five miles outside Shanghai. It was a fully immersive, self-contained world for experimental athletic equipment: base layers and outerwear, of course, but also responsive textiles that could sense hypothermia and receive updates to Nike's spacewear line, now worn by so many travelers embarking for the deep cold of Mars and beyond. Marte, just 19 years old but already the best downhill skier in the world, was the first outside visitor ever to be invited to see the complex.

They stepped through the door, boots crunching deep into artificial snow, entering a space so vast it would be wrong to describe it as a room. Officially, this was the largest architectural interior on Earth. Powerful winds blew down from disguised vents in the walls, and as Marte turned to follow the hurricane-like whirls of snow, she realized that she could not see the ceiling. Somewhere high above her were powerful weather machines so far away and so clouded by atmospheric effects, they remained invisible.

Taylor urged her onward. They hiked together through thickets of trees, roots fed from below by nutrient-rich geotextiles, and branches dosed with regular cycles of UV light. They ascended hills and scrambled up the sides of artificial boulders, the landscape around them accumulating fresh snow. The terrain looked for all the world like a wilderness trail somewhere back home in Norway, but Marte could not shake the uncanny knowledge that they were inside a building just a brief metro ride from Shanghai's international airport.

It was as if Taylor had read her mind. "If you're inside a room so big you can't see the walls," he asked, his breath forming puffs of fog, "are you still really inside?"

The question dominated Marte's thoughts as they walked along the edge of a full-scale forest — Marte brushed her fingertips against pine needles and rocks, as if to reassure herself they were real — coming to a small clearing in which an electric vehicle waited up ahead. It looked like a snowcat but was colored like an athletic shoe, covered in dynamic shapes and patterns, a hyper-pink Nike logo clearly visible on both sides. They hopped in.

A few minutes later, they crested a large hill, and their driver signaled to Taylor. "You're going to want to see this," he said. He moved aside to share the view.

Visible through the windshield was an entire valley. Snow-covered peaks roared with wind in the distance. It seemed impossible — a building so vast it held mountains, cliffs, distant plateaus, and forests. Marte saw deer grazing beneath fully grown pine trees. She actually laughed; she could not believe what she was seeing.

Finally, their destination. From the outside, it appeared to be nothing more than a rustic cabin, its walls made from axe-hewn logs, smoke rising from a stone chimney — a digital effect, Marte would learn, relying on magnetically charged air, being trialed ahead of its public debut.

Inside, the facility's landscape architect and Taylor's team of weather-machine technicians met them. Articles of clothing Marte was not allowed to photograph hung on the walls, and in the center of the room, a full-scale holographic model of the complex flickered to life.

Over cups of tea, Marte's hosts showed her the topography of future athletic events, where all the hills, slopes, and trails would be. One valley, they said, was even designed to mimic the landscape on Mars, where so many tourists were headed. They handed her insulated gloves thinner than paper but impossible to pierce, so warm she couldn't wear them inside for more than a few minutes. At one point, they pulled a rod of temperature-resistant metal out of a freezer. Intended for ski poles, though able to be scaled up for use in architecture, it had been chilled to negative 50 degrees. Marte, amazed, could handle it with her bare hands.

Taylor glanced at the screen on his wrist and sat forward. They were running late. "Our lift is waiting," he said. "We should go."

Marte nodded, still a bit speechless, struggling to take it all in. Through the window, she watched snow howling over rock masses in the distance and saw what appeared to be birds of prey circling mature fir trees.

"I'm excited to hear your feedback," said the landscape architect as they stepped back out into the snow. Their next stop would be a chairlift, taking them up — and up and up — to experience the terrain firsthand. "I designed the slopes in a way an athlete like you will appreciate," he said. "But if you don't like them, even the mountains are adjustable."

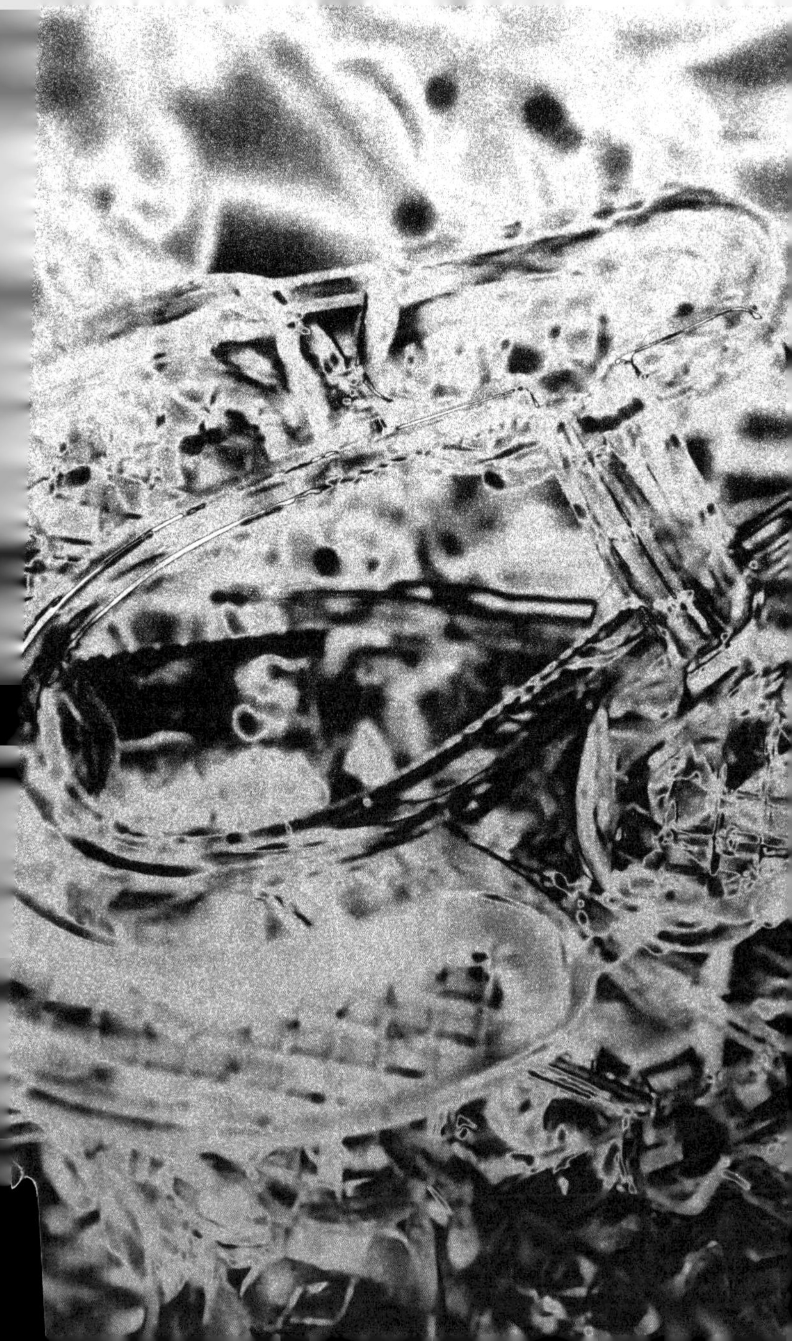

Picture Credits

1 NASA Johnson Space Center
2–3 Paola Kudacki
15 Ensign John Gay/U.S. Navy
16–17 NASA/JPL-Caltech
20 Cover of *Jogging*, January 1967/Grosset & Dunlap
21 China Daily/REUTERS
23 Paola Kudacki
24 The British Museum
26 Shutterstock
33 Elise Amendola/AP/Shutterstock
34 Google Earth
41 Paola Kudacki
46 Summit Medical and Scientific
49 Veli Granö
53 deep3dstudio
56 Found imagery
62 The British Museum
63 Found imagery
67 AFP
68–69 Center for Disease Control and Prevention
70–71 Christopher Stippich, MD
74–75 Found imagery
78 Paola Kudacki
83 Found imagery
85 Tony Duffy/Getty Images Europe
96 Carl Eberth/documenta archiv
98–99 Hart Lëshkina
105 Stock photo/Getty Images
106–107 Found imagery
112 Mario Klingemann
114–115 ABB Group
119 Dan Little/HRL Laboratorles
120–121 Found imagery
124 Found imagery

130 Found imagery
132–133 NASA/JPL-Caltech/ASU
135 Paul Crock/AFP/Getty Images
137 Scott Bauer/U.S. Department of Agriculture
145 Graeme Walker
146 Found imagery
148 Brian Kane
151 Cover of the *Whole Earth Catalog*, March 1970
152–153 Bertrand Piccard
154 Emory Kristof/National Geographic
160 *Science*, Vol 326, 2 October 2009
163 Los Alamos National Laboratory
164 Found imagery
169 Paola Kudacki
170–171 Keystone France/Getty Images
172 Boris Horvat/AFP/Getty Images
174–175 Science Photo Library
177 Found imagery
178 Bele Olmez/Getty Images
181 Jonathan Blair/*National Geographic*
184 *Astrophysical Journal*, 734:10, 10

All other images courtesy Nike.

Illustrations
57, 87, 125, 155, 185 Bráulio Amado

Every reasonable effort has been made to acknowledge the ownership of copyright for images included in this book. Any errors or omissions that may have occurred are inadvertent and will be corrected in subsequent editions provided notification is sent to the publisher.

Select Bibliography

Eames, Ray. Draft speech, U.S.-Japan Conference on Cultural and Educational Interchange, Tokyo, July 1978. Container I:218: Folder 13, Charles and Ray Eames Papers, Manuscript Division, Library of Congress, Washington, D.C.

Nelson, George. *George Nelson On Design*. Whitney Library of Design, 1979.

Sagan, Carl. *Pale Blue Dot: A Vision of the Human Future in Space*. Random House, 1994.

Schneier, Bruce. *Click Here to Kill Everybody: Security and Survival in a Hyper-connected World*. W. W. Norton & Company, 2018.

Tanizaki, Junichiro. *In Praise of Shadows*. Leete's Island Books, 1977.

Acknowledgements

This book would not be possible without the generous contributions of Volkan Alkanoglu, Rob Barnette, Tom Clarke, Ron Faris, Sarah Hammond, Seana Hannah, John Hoke, Jalaj Hora, Jonathan Johnsongriffin, Eric King, Ratnakar Lavu, Sally Lohan, Jay Meschter, Noah Murphy-Reinhertz, Matt Nurse, Liz Rodgers, and Mike Vedomske. Special thanks to Sara Blasing, John Hoke, Mary Remuzzi, and Mark Rhodes for their unfailing belief in and support of this project.